Wogan's
Ireland

A tour around the country that made the man

Terry Wogan

SIMON &
SCHUSTER
ILLUSTRATED

London · New York · Sydney · Toronto · New Delhi

A CBS COMPANY

First published in Great Britain by
Simon & Schuster UK Ltd, 2011

A CBS COMPANY

Copyright © 2011 Terry Wogan

Based on the programme
Terry Wogan's Ireland created by
Presentable Limited for the BBC and
licensed to Simon & Schuster UK
Limited by Zodiak Rights Limited

zodiak
rights

1 3 5 7 9 10 8 6 4 2

SIMON & SCHUSTER
ILLUSTRATED BOOKS
Simon & Schuster UK Ltd
222 Gray's Inn Road
London WC1X 8HB

www.simonandschuster.co.uk

Simon & Schuster Australia, Sydney

Simon & Schuster India, New Delhi

Editorial director: **Francine Lawrence**
Design: **Richard Proctor and**
 Geoff Fennell
Picture researcher: **Emma O'Neill**
Map artwork: **KJA-artists.com**
Production manager: **Katherine**
 Thornton
Commercial director: **Ami Richards**

A CIP catalogue record for this book
is available from the British Library

ISBN 978-0-85720-351-9

Printed and bound in Spain
Colour reproduction by Dot Gradations

Country road,
Beara Peninsula,
County Cork

The ramble

I've started...

The word 'journey' has become as abused as 'celebrity' so, if you're coming on this trip with me, I'd rather you looked upon it as more of a meander, a dawdle if you will, over the four green fields of Erin. And, before we start, I don't want any talk from those of you who may have enjoyed the delights of Ireland already. It's a big little island and my clockwise tour – inspired by the BBC television programme *Terry Wogan's Ireland* – is a circumnavigation, beginning and ending in the fair city of Dublin. Two hours of television will only skim the surface, but this book allows me the freedom to include reminiscences, from my boyhood and young adulthood, of other magical places – the Skelligs, Dingle Bay, the Clare coast, the Aran Islands and the rest – that we were unable to visit during filming.

In the time we had making *Terry Wogan's Ireland*, I stored up enough memories to last several lifetimes: Mícheál, the boatman of Clear Island, making everyone a cup of tea under the watchful gaze of the great Fastnet Lighthouse, on a mercifully calm Atlantic, shimmering like silk... Enniskerry, County Wicklow – one of Ireland's prettiest villages – where my father was born in the shadow of Sugar Loaf Mountain. The Da ran away from it, at fifteen, for many reasons, among them 'you couldn't eat the scenery'.

The great estate of Powerscourt, where his lordship lived in pomp and dug a sunken road along the front of the house so that he and his good lady might not be troubled by the sight of his labourers coming to work... The little harbours of Portmagee and Baltimore, a delight to the eye and the spirit as I pulled back my bedroom curtains... The grandeur of Killarney's lakes, even more dramatic when shrouded in dark, lowering clouds... The swans on the Shannon at Limerick; the little house there where I spent my first fifteen years.

The crossing of the border from the Republic into Northern Ireland... The only reason you know that you've crossed the line are the road signs changing from kilometres to miles. The armed soldiers and police are no more, the gun emplacements and the watchtowers replaced by 'bureaux de change' where Ireland's euros may be exchanged for sterling.

Belfast, a place I only visited in my youth for the purposes of being kicked around a rugby field, with that huge sad hole in the docks, where they built, and from where they launched, the unsinkable *Titanic*... Walking the walls of Derry in the driving rain while my friend, the broadcaster Gerry Anderson, explained that in Northern Ireland it wasn't the side of the tracks you were born that made the difference but the side of the river... The sun shone on Lough Erne when Father Brian D'Arcy showed us the beauties of that great lake and told us of its place in Ireland's history. A place for reflection... As they say here, 'When God made time, he made plenty of it.'

But we seemed to be always on the move – the Hill of Tara, walking the very land from where the High Kings of Ireland could survey the extent of their power from Dublin Bay in the south, to the Mountains of Mourne looking northward... The ancient burial mounds of Brú na Bóinne, perhaps older than the Pyramids...

'Bóinne' is the Irish for the Boyne, in which river's valley the only significant battle in international terms ever fought on Irish soil ended in victory for William of Orange, and the defeat of James Stuart and the Catholic Jacobites. Hundreds of years later,

The song begins:
'Oh, Mary, this London's a wonderful sight'...
Yet goes on to say:
'But for all that I found there I might as well be Where the Mountains of Mourne sweep down to the sea.'

they still march to the drums in Northern Ireland, in memory of the great Protestant victory.

In Malahide, another pretty harbour town just outside Dublin, there is a castle that once belonged to the Wogan family, where, it is said, twelve men sat down to breakfast on the morning of the Battle of the Boyne. None ever returned…

So many memories, and so much more: the brave naked ladies of Sligo; Galway's Spanish past; meeting schoolmates of long ago… But here, if we're going to make this 'journey' together, you'd better get on your walking boots, there's lots to see. And bring a raincoat!

I've started…

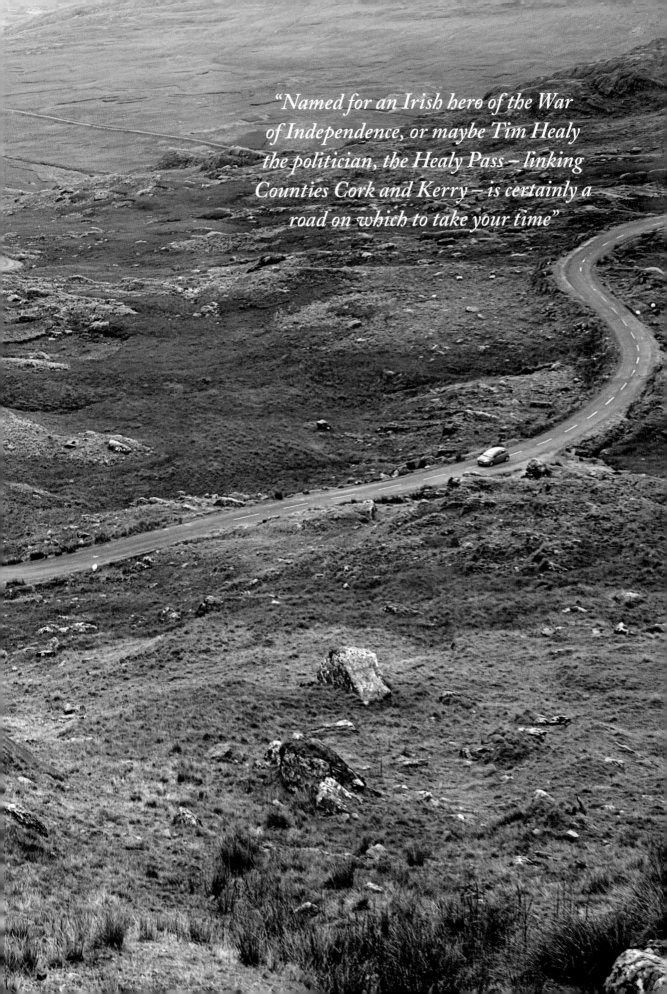

"*Named for an Irish hero of the War of Independence, or maybe Tim Healy the politician, the Healy Pass – linking Counties Cork and Kerry – is certainly a road on which to take your time*"

Holyhead to Dun Laoghaire

It was entirely right and proper that I begin my circumnavigation of Ireland from Holyhead in Anglesey, North Wales. A beautiful day, entirely appropriate to Snowdonia National Park, with its hills and valleys, its little rivers sparkling in the sunshine. Even more appropriately, I'm taking the Swedish ferry, luxurious successor to the rough old mail boat that plied for so many years, back and forth across the Irish Sea: Dun Laoghaire to Holyhead, Holyhead to Dun Laoghaire. That old mail boat carried hundreds of years of tears and sorrow, hopes and dreams of a better life, for hundreds of thousands of emigrating Irish men and women. Holyhead was their first view of a foreign shore. With what apprehension, and fear mixed with excitement, would they have first stepped on to the soil of Anglesey island?

The view to Howth Head, northeast of Dublin city, from the port of Dun Laoghaire

I made that journey once myself, when but a slip of a lad, in the early fifties, in order to see Ireland play England at Twickenham. A long, tedious journey, not helped by a rough Irish Sea causing me to throw up all over my new suede shoes. It wasn't a journey I'd want to repeat in a hurry, and it's taken fifty years for me to try it again. This time, I'm going in the opposite direction, leaving Holyhead and Anglesey on the first leg of my return to Ireland. I'll confess to a frisson of excitement: what will I find there – a new Ireland, a country and its people changed from all I left behind forty years ago?

There's a historical precedent for my leaving for Ireland from here, too. Wogan is a Welsh name, derived from 'Gwgn', freely translated as 'glum'. However morose my ancestors were, they prospered in the eleventh and twelfth centuries under their Norman conquerors. From the records, it appears that you couldn't throw a stone in a Welsh country road without hitting a Wogan knight. And as we'll see later on, if you're still with me, chevaliers and barons in France also bore the proud Wogan name. How my great-grandfather plied his trade as a bootmaker and roofer hundreds of years on, we'll also get to later…

The brave Baron de Wogan, togged out for the worst of the Canadian winter in the grizzly-bear suit he made himself. Or is it the Abominable Snowman?

THE BARON DE WOGAN.

Dun Laoghaire, genteel seaside town and for many years the major port of entry for people arriving from Britain. Also the place where Queen Victoria first stepped on Irish soil

The first recorded Wogan in Irish history arrived, with a bunch of Norman roughnecks, in the middle of the twelfth century, at the invitation of the treacherous King of Leinster, who wanted their help to gain the kingship of Ireland. The Normans, as they proved not only in Britain but all over Europe, were not descended from the Vikings for nothing, and knocked seven bells out of everybody so successfully that in 1155 Pope Adrian granted the lordship of Ireland to Henry II of England, so that 'he might bring the trust of the Christian faith to the ignorant and rude Irish'. This in flagrant disregard of the fact that it was the scholarship and missionary zeal of Irish monks that had, almost alone, kept the Christian faith, its art and literature, alive during the Dark Ages after the fall of the Roman Empire. Mind you, Adrian was the only English pope in history.

It was Sir John Wogan who joined the Norman invaders, as 'justiciar', a role which seemed to cover everything from the law to the exchequer. In common with his fellow conquerors, he

I recognise some of these hooligans in Belvedere College yard, but that's not me in the short trousers... I spent two and a half happy years at Belvedere, before embarking on my briefly brilliant banking career

took what he wanted, building castles, one in Meath, Clongowes Wood, which became a distinguished Jesuit public school, and another by the sea near Dublin, at Malahide. And like the rest of the Normans, he eventually, as Irish history tells us, 'became more Irish than the Irish themselves'.

The huge ferry churns away from Holyhead, into a suspiciously calm, sunlit Irish Sea. We sail along with a smoothness unknown in the old mail boat, and at twice the speed. Then, we stop. The Irish Sea is not to be treated in this cavalier fashion, and it has responded with a sea mist. I'm reminded of the mythology of the Celtic sea god, Manannán mac Lir, who regularly protected his dominion with impenetrable fog, particularly his kingdom of Tír na nÓg, the Land of the Young, known nowadays as the Isle of Man, which still carries the great sea god's name.

The mist eventually lifts and, soon, there it stands before us – Dun Laoghaire harbour, and Ireland...

Dun Laoghaire, pronounced 'Done Leary', looks more of a genteel English seaside town than anything Irish. The Edwardian houses sweep elegantly down to the harbour, there's a promenade and a bandstand. And in prime position, the Royal Irish Yacht Club. Of course, the old place has changed, with the passing of the mail boat and the arrival of the huge ferries, but I detect

Malahide Castle, just outside Dublin, once the Wogan family seat

echoes of the old order here still, the place where Queen Victoria first stepped on Irish soil. She was well received by the loyal Irish of Dublin, although W.B. Yeats deliberately turned his back on her carriage, and the rebel Maud Gonne MacBride pointedly wore a black veil. Which, you'll agree, was certainly showing her. It's not recorded whether Queen Victoria noticed.

I spent a gentle two weeks in Dun Laoghaire in the early stages of my banking career, without throwing the accounts

The promenade at Dun Laoghaire, a favourite spot for a Dubliner's weekend stroll – and for a boy broadcaster momentarily escaping the studios of Radio Éireann for a blast of bracing sea air

into too much confusion, and when the present Lady Wogan and I were first married, we lived in a little dormer bungalow on Killiney Hill, overlooking the harbour and Dublin Bay. If you walked to the top of Killiney Hill, a splendid view of the other side of the bay stretched before you, to the Wicklow Mountains and the imposing Sugar Loaf, but I'm getting ahead of myself – all of that, and my ancestral roots, lie before us, so don't say that you haven't been warned.

When but a boy broadcaster with Irish radio, Radio Éireann, in the longueurs between continuity announcing and news-reading, a fellow tyro, Andy O'Mahony, and I would take the road from the studios in Henry Street, Dublin, in my trusty Morris Minor with the broken passenger seat, to walk the promenade at Dun Laoghaire. The alternative was to cross narrow Henry Street to Madigan's pub, directly opposite the entrance to Radio Éireann, a well-beaten track. Andy and I, spoiled bank clerks both, preferred the bracing sea air to a pint of the black stuff, at least before lunch.

One day, returning to the continuity suite, suitably fresh-faced, Andy opened the microphone, made an announcement, and carefully started a musical interlude with a record on one of the turntables on the desk. He then turned to me and we continued our erudite discourse. After a couple of minutes, obviously irritated by his thesis being interrupted by the music, he absent-mindedly turned, took the needle off the record and returned to our discussion. Ireland, or at least the part of it listening to the national radio station, was plunged into silence. God knows how many people all over the country thought that the end of the world was nigh, or at best, the electricity cut off. Or maybe they even threw their wirelesses at the wall in frustration, before I gently pointed out to Andy the error of his ways, and once again the plangent notes of the Tulla Céilí Band were heard throughout the land.

"The mail boat – how many hopes, dreams and tears it carried across the Irish Sea to Britain. The steamer Cambria *in Dun Laoghaire harbour in the 1950s"*

BELFAST

DUBLIN
DUN LAOGHAIRE

Dun Laoghaire to Dublin

From Dun Laoghaire it's but a jaunt to the heart of Dublin city, although Dave, our doughty driver, spent the time bemoaning the dreadful traffic. I promised that one day I'd take him down Regent Street and Soho in London, and then, as an added bonus, for a restful half-day in the stationary chaos of the M25 motorway, if he *really* wanted to see traffic.

St Stephen's Green is a peaceful oasis, a park of trees and flowers and water at the top of Dublin's most fashionable street, Grafton Street, 'a wonderland' according to the Irish actor Noel Purcell's popular song of the fifties. And so it still is. The Ma and Da met while working in a grocery store, Leverett & Frye, in Grafton Street. He was behind the counter with the comestibles, she was in the cash. Their eyes met over the bacon slicer, he was

The bandstand in the peaceful setting of St Stephen's Green, Dublin, a stone's throw from the hustle and bustle of Grafton Street

offered the managership of the Limerick branch, they got married, and… but I'm racing ahead of myself again…

Off Grafton Street is a much smaller thoroughfare, King Street. And on King Street is a lovely old music hall, the Gaiety Theatre. This theatre holds so many memories: as a member of the Rathmines and Rathgar Musical and Dramatic Society, I trod the boards here in not only a Gilbert and Sullivan operetta but *Bitter Sweet, Love From Judy* and many another crowd-pleasing musical extravaganza. Amateur dramatics was big in Ireland then. The Brother, Brian, for instance, was a fine actor. Unfortunately, there wasn't enough professional acting work available to make it a career.

Ah, the Gaiety, where I tripped the light fantastic in amateur musical comedy and presented my first Eurovision Song Contest in 1971

Amid the rock 'n' rolling of the fifties, a friend, Ken Daly – with whom I'd shared the sweat and tears of the Belvedere College rugby front row – and I somehow developed a love of opera. Every year in the Gaiety Theatre, the Dublin Grand Opera Society stages a season of Italian opera, flying in producers, conductors, designers and stars from the great Italian opera houses, while providing their own chorus and extras, or 'supers', as we were known. Because that's how Ken and I got in for nothing to enjoy the finest operas – we signed on as waiters in *La Traviata*, casual Venetians in *Otello*, Assyrian slaves in *Aida*. We certainly got a better view than even the exalted customers in the Grand Circle, although in the case of *Aida* it did involve wearing a loincloth and smearing ourselves in some brown muck, as we were lashed by cruel oppressors. Talk about sacrificing yourself for your art…

Dave the driver, a typical Dubliner – a constant source of good humour, wit and sharp comment

Your man in **The Gondoliers,** *Belvedere College, Dublin, when he and the world were young...*

I have to admit that my performances were for one season only, having left a little to be desired in the eyes of the Italian producer. Perhaps it was my anachronistic wearing of suede shoes, as a waiter in the '*Libiamo*' drinking scene of *La Traviata*, or, as a priest, enjoying a pint in the green room and failing to turn up for the Easter hymn procession in *Cavalleria Rusticana* – or was that *Pagliacci*? Either way, it signalled the end of my brief hour upon the grand opera stage, but far from the finish of my King Street days.

It was in the Gaiety Theatre that I made my debut as a

commentator at the Eurovision Song Contest. I'd barely begun to make any impression on the British listening public when BBC Radio asked me to return to Ireland in 1971 to do the Eurovision. Given the grandiose magnificence, the Himalayan heights to which the Song Contest has risen in the intervening years, it almost beggars belief that it was staged by Radio Telefís Éireann in a music hall that had room for fewer than a thousand people by the time you crammed in cameras, sound, lighting, stage crews, orchestra, commentary boxes and all the other paraphernalia for what was, even then, the major European Broadcasting Union event of the year. I have a vague recollection of Clodagh Rodgers singing her heart out for Le Royaume-Uni, but who sang for Ireland, and who won, is lost in the mists of time. Not that it makes too much difference today, either.

And guess what's about to open at the Gaiety Theatre, Dublin, this week? Only *Riverdance*! *Riverdance*, that extraordinary explosion of drum, pipe and the hammering of hard-shoe Irish dancing, the fiercely dramatic interlude in the 1994 Eurovision Song Contest that put all the competing nations and their songs in the shade, making everything else irrelevant, and creating the outstanding memory in the Song Contest's history. I don't think

Man about town leans casually against his family's first car

Pronounced Portmarnick, the lovely beach was the usual destination for the Wogan family Sunday afternoon spin in the new car

it's too strong to say that it was with *Riverdance* that Ireland announced its place in Europe, that *Riverdance* was the first time the Celtic Tiger roared.

Moya Doherty and John McColgan were two young people I'd met in London, when both were working in television there – Moya as presenter, John as producer. They went back to work for Irish television, Moya becoming a director/producer. And she's the one who produced the 1994 Eurovision from the huge Point arena in Dublin and, of course, *Riverdance*. We sat in the Gaiety and talked of old times, and the extraordinary international success that this spectacle of Irish music and dance continues to enjoy all over the world. They'd just returned from a triumph in the Great Hall of the People in Tiananmen Square, Beijing. *Riverdance* might have just faded away into the mists of time, a memory of one fierce few minutes, without the masterly direction of Moya and John.

That commitment, that constant attention to quality and detail, is what keeps the musical phenomenon fresh and alive. As evidence, Moya Doherty took me to Portmarnock, a Dublin

suburb by the sea, and we enjoyed the toe-tapping brilliance of future Riverdancers. A revelation, just as the show was to those of us for whom Irish dancing was for sissies; rigid, formalised, with no upper body movement, arms stiffly held by the sides to hold down the short skirt, in case anybody should see your knickers.

Portmarnock was where the Da would take us for a Sunday spin in the big Ford Consul. We didn't have a car in Limerick, relying on the generosity of those better placed in life than ourselves. The Da having risen to dizzy heights, we graciously joined him, as he drove to Portmarnock's lovely, great beach, and

Country club, Portmarnock. The happy couple and proud parents, Tim and Ellie Joyce and Rose and Michael Wogan, forty-six years ago...

watched as he hurled a line into the sea, in the usually fruitless search for bass or flounder. Even if we caught one, it went back in the sea. The Ma didn't do fish.

Portmarnock, or, to be more specific, the country club there, was where Helen and I had our wedding reception. Quite a drive from the church in Rathmines where the marriage took place, in the rain. This surprised nobody and certainly didn't in any way upset the cheery attitude of the crowd who joined the wedding party inside the church and, standing on the seats and benches, cheered and applauded the happy, bemused couple as we made our way, man and wife, into a life together that has, so far, lasted forty-five years. The rain cleared off for the reception, not that anyone noticed, well inoculated as they were by the free bar, a generous gesture by Helen's father, Tim, who got his money's worth by making at least three speeches at the wedding breakfast. One of them was in the middle of my own father's speech, which didn't go down too well as far as the Da was concerned, but was hardly noticed, in view of the fact that people seemed to be walking in off the street to add their few well-chosen words.

One of the reasons for my making this pilgrimage was to see how much things had changed in Ireland since I'd been away. Portmarnock had certainly changed, in the way I was to find most Irish towns, big and small, had changed. The evidence of Ireland's prosperity during the boom years, when the Tiger roared, is everywhere to be seen, with housing developments sprawling in all directions over what used to be green fields and seeming to choke what I remembered as quiet suburbs. Later, on my way through the rural county town, I would see far more depressing evidence of a property boom that went bust – rows of unfinished developments, housing estates half-built and abandoned as developers and builders ran out of money and the banks, too late, saw the error of their profligate lending ways. The unpaid workers had laid down their tools and left. A modern Irish tragedy, in a country that, historically, has had more than its share.

"County Wicklow – they call it 'The Garden of Ireland'. The view from Sugar Loaf Mountain"

Dublin to Enniskerry

Enniskerry is less than an hour from Dublin, at least at the speed Dave drives, and the Wicklow hills, in the shadow of Sugar Loaf Mountain, and enjoys a reputation as one of Ireland's prettiest places. It was to this little town that Michael Wogan, my great-grandfather, came in the early nineteenth century, to try his luck as a bootmaker. Don't ask how a descendant of knights, chevaliers, lords of the manor and French baronetcies ended up repairing boots – this is not a history lesson. I can tell you that the old boy abandoned the boot business in favour of roofing, but only because Oona Wogan, a distant relative – proud possessor of what she termed 'the tall Wogan gene' and chronicler of the family history, with particular reference to Enniskerry – told me so, and produced the old photographs to prove it. There's a real beauty,

One of Ireland's loveliest villages – Enniskerry, where my father was born

taken in 1901, of Viscount Wingfield, Lord Powerscourt, his lady and his family, on the steps of Powerscourt House, with the Protestant vicar, the Catholic priest and his lordship's tenants, the good burghers of Enniskerry. And there he is, third row from the front, Michael Wogan, bootmaker/roofer to the gentry, sporting a beard that rivals the good lord's magnificent growth.

The magnificent estate of Powerscourt, with its sweeping balustrades, terraces and great stone steps leading to its Italianate gardens, with their fountains, and Sugar Loaf Mountain as the icing on the cake, had fallen into sad decay the last time I visited, but the grandeur has been restored and nowadays the great house is a major tourist attraction. In the days of great-grandfather Wogan, and, indeed, in my own father's young manhood, without the Big House and the employment it provided Enniskerry could scarcely

Powerscourt House and gardens. A burnt-out ruin last time I visited, now restored to its former glory and a major tourist attraction. Imagine: people eating ice-cream on his lordship's terrace!

have existed. Almost all the inhabitants of the village relied on Lord Powerscourt's grace and favour as his servants, victuallers, retailers, labourers, gardeners, farmers and, yes, bootmakers and roofers. I'm pleased to say that there's still a Wingfield descendant in residence at Powerscourt, but the feudalism that helped to drive my father away from the place is long gone.

The relics of 'ould decency' can still be seen: in front of the entrance to the Great House is a sunken road, specially dug on the orders of a past Lord Powerscourt so that he and his good lady might not be disturbed by the sight of their servants and labourers coming to work in the mornings.

It was fascinating to meet my hitherto unknown relations and share their interest, their painstaking research into the Wogans of Church Hill, Enniskerry, County Wicklow, but my Da, Michael Thomas, born there in 1901, didn't share this affection, couldn't wait to get out of the place, and although he brought me there, on a couple of occasions, to meet his sisters and my first cousins, even then I knew that his heart wasn't in it. As he always said, pretty and all as the surroundings were, 'you couldn't eat the scenery', and times, as they invariably were in rural Ireland, were hard. His father, another Michael, was mentioned in despatches in the *Freeman's Journal* for heroic work during 'The Great Fire' of 1894 that burned down the village's only hostelry, the Powerscourt Arms, but he never was a hero to my father. The Da adored his mother, and spoke of her frequently – his father, he never talked about. He did talk, and freely, about his resentment at having to step off the pavement to accommodate Enniskerry's ruling junta of parish priest, schoolteacher and police sergeant. As

I wonder what great-grandfather Michael would think of his descendant walking around the place as if he owned it…?

for his lordship, he rarely visited his fiefdom, and my father reciprocated by not visiting Powerscourt. Not that he would have been let through the gates, anyway.

According to the Da, he walked barefoot to school in all weathers, and uphill both ways. Although he claimed to have been expelled for attempting to take the teacher's head off with a slate while still but a child, since he could read freely, write in a meticulous fist and do his sums, I would assume that whether he left in a marked manner or not, he took the high road to the seaside town of Bray, and a new career as a grocer's 'curate', when he was about fifteen. And where did he learn to read music, sing operatic arias and play the violin? The Da preferred to tell of the hard times, living above the grocer's shop, and up at all hours with deliveries and tying up bags of sugar.

Very occasionally, he would tell of happy days in the Wicklow Mountains, fishing on Lough Dan, and when the mood took him for a longer Sunday spin in the Consul, we'd join the hundreds of Dublin residents who walked and picnicked among the heather-covered, barren hills. I loved it – the rocks, the ice-cold lakes, the lemonade, the corned-beef sandwiches. Helen Joyce that was, and who subsequently became known as 'Ireland's Luckiest Woman' through a fortuitous marriage, was another whose family took to

Cousin Oona points out the picture, hanging proudly in the local pub, of Lord Powerscourt and his fiefs

The old bootmaker/roofer himself, great-grandfather Michael

the hills on a Sunday, after Mass. However, her father, Tim, was not a man who was prepared to leave the comfort of his own fireside for a cold collation. Not for him the lemonade or sandwich. Sunday lunch was a three-course meal, and served piping hot. A Primus stove, with all its attendant difficulties, had to be lit and, upon it, cooked soup, boiled bacon, cabbage and potatoes.

Tim Joyce, no more than my Da, served his time as a grocer's assistant and, like my father, with hard work and intelligence went on to greater things, building a better life for his family. In his eighties, Tim planted some small apple trees in his back garden, fully expecting to pick their fruit in the fullness of time. Which he did. He died at ninety-three, still refusing streaky bacon, boiling his cabbage to liquid extinction, and insisting on his soup being cooled on the kitchen windowsill.

Lord and Lady Powerscourt on the steps of their grand house, graciously allowing themselves to be photographed with the loyal villagers of Enniskerry. Only Michael Wogan has dared to match his lordship's beard…

RIGHT: *The Bray branch of that fine purveyor of comestibles, Leverett & Frye, pre World War One. See – I'm not making this all up*

"Among the Wicklow hills, Lough Dan –
where the Da caught many a trout
– shimmers in the distance"

BELFAST

DUBLIN
Enniskerry

CORK

Enniskerry to Cork

We've a long drive ahead of us. From the barren Wicklow Mountains, we head south, bypassing the 'sunny south-east' coast that proudly proclaims itself as the country's best-weather region. That's as maybe. I can only tell you that, flying once from Luton airport to Cork, we touched down in Waterford, and I've never seen so many people look half-drowned as they struggled through the driving rain to join the plane. My other memory of Waterford is the fog that enveloped the helicopter that was taking me to Dublin for a meeting with the then Taoiseach (prime minister), the infamous Charlie Haughey. I'd been hosting a charity 'celeb-am' golf day at Waterford Golf Club, in, it must be admitted, lovely weather, and the bold Charlie had expressed a desire to meet me. And indeed, since one of his sons had a

The town of Cobh, County Cork. From the Great Famine onwards, it was from this port that countless Irish men, women and children left to seek a better life in America

helicopter company that was helping to ferry our 'celebs' back and forth, I hopped aboard for the trip to Dublin.

Unfortunately, the Celtic mist had closed in by the time we started, but the Taoiseach was not to be disappointed, and off we went, flying so low that we could easily have had the horns off a tall cow. When we hit a tree, wiser counsels, having let off high-pitched screams of panic, decided that we should head back to Waterford. Not to land safely and wait for the fog to lift – this is Ireland. The pilot found the railway line to Dublin and followed

The front page of Harper's Weekly, *28 February 1880, depicting 'Ireland' standing on the cliffs signalling to America for help, while a starving family huddles behind her*

it all the way to the capital. The Taoiseach was pleased to see me, but not half as pleased as I was, having been convinced I would never see home and mother again.

Charlie Haughey was hospitality itself, pouring me a pint from his own pub bar and showing me around his home, strewn with pictures of himself with the world's great and good. And there, beside a photo of himself and Margaret Thatcher, was a finely carved wooden harp bearing the legend, 'To Charlie, from all the boys at Long Kesh.' The 'boys' being members of the IRA, interned there. Charlie Haughey was a rascal, a throwback to the Irish Tammany Hall politicians of New York. He owned an island off Cork, a boat, kept a mistress, liked silk shirts from Paris and lived a champagne lifestyle that he couldn't possibly have afforded on a prime minister's salary. The Irish, who have always resented authority, for good historical reasons, had a sneaking regard for those, like Charlie, who bucked the system. Whether they still have any regard for any politician these days is debatable.

Philomena O'Shea recalls the sadness of her emigration in the hungry 1950s. She is one of the very few ever to return to Ireland

We never got to Wexford on this trip, either, another county that has played its part in the country's history. It was here that the first successful invaders of Ireland, the Normans, landed, with your man, Wogan, bringing up the rear. In no time, they'd bent

the bemused natives to their will and built their castles, all in line in sight of each other in case any Irish eejit thought of creating trouble. I know the Norman keep of Bargy Castle, because it's the ancestral home of my friend, the singer/songwriter Chris de Burgh. A Norman name, if ever there was one. When I was last there, the flag flying from the tower bore the same markings as that flown in Jerusalem by a de Burgh during the Crusades. And just have an educated guess where Chris de Burgh and his family live these days… Enniskerry.

Starting with the Normans, Ireland and the Irish endured centuries of colonisation, oppression, rebellion, with its consequent aftermath of cruel repression and religious discrimination. But nothing to compare with the national tragedy that was the Great Famine. The potato was the staple food of poverty-stricken Irish peasants, a third of the population relied upon it, and in 1845 it was struck by a blight. 'An Gorta Mór', the Great Hunger, began. By the time it was finished, in 1852, one million people had died, and Ireland had lost a quarter of its population to starvation and emigration. The famine has left an irreparable mark demographically, culturally and politically on Irish life ever since. The failures

Father Mathew, founder of the 'Pioneers'. I, too, pledged never to touch the demon drink…I held out until I was seventeen

Ah, around the great bar of the old Hi-B, with mine host, Brian O'Donnell. I didn't let on that I had a mobile phone about my person

LEFT: *Cobh marina and Jeanne Rynhart's statue of fourteen-year-old Annie Moore – the first person to be registered through immigration at Ellis Island, New York – and her two younger brothers*

of a British government, which allowed the export of wheat while a people starved, are well documented elsewhere, but any view of Ireland cannot ignore the terrible famine and its aftermath.

So, my journey must take me to Cork, or, more specifically, to its port of Cobh (pronounced 'Cove'), the second largest natural harbour in the world. Nowadays, it's a natural berth for great cruise liners and, indeed, the ill-fated *Titanic* paused here, before continuing its deadly journey. Cobh, during the Great Famine and for the next hundred years, was Ireland's emergency exit. In those years, two and a half million people left the country from here, into the unknown, for what they hoped was a better life. Cobh was their final sight of their sad, hungry land. Their last sight, for the great majority never returned.

I was delighted to meet one who did, Philomena O'Shea, who was just seventeen when, in 1952, she decided to leave her family behind and seek in America the work she couldn't find in Ireland. By then, at least the ships were not the death traps of the previous hundred years. Philomena remembers bunk beds and six to a cabin, and coming up on deck in the morning for a last, sad, lonely goodbye. She was from a small village in Kerry, and the loneliness and homesickness didn't leave her for a year. But in Springfield, Massachusetts, she met another immigrant from Kerry, William O'Shea. They married, had a daughter, William came into the family farm back home, the O'Sheas moved back to Kerry, had

six more children, and now all that worries Philomena is that her grandchildren may have to take the emigrant route again...

From Ireland's past of hopes and tears, down the road to the second city of the Republic, Cork, as the song has it, 'On the Banks of My Own Lovely Lee'. Drink used to flow through Cork almost as freely as the River Lee; the city at one time had at least 800 licensed premises. So it's no wonder that it was from here that the great temperance reformer, Father Mathew, began his Herculean task of prising the Irish away from the demon drink. A statue to the great man stands proudly on Cork's main thoroughfare, and rightly so, for in the nineteenth century and well into the

The Republic's second city, where flows the 'lovely Lee' and Shandon's bells call all Corkonians to prayer

twentieth, the good father had persuaded half the adult population to take the pledge and forswear the booze forever. You wore a little badge, called a 'pioneer pin', to show the world that lips that touched liquor would never touch yours. In my case, the pledge lasted until I was all of seventeen. It didn't last all that long for the rest of the population either – by 2003, Ireland had the second largest alcohol consumption per capita in the world.

It's only fitting that we drop into Cork's most famous watering hole, the little Hi-B. Brian O'Donnell is the landlord and proprietor of this most eccentric of pubs, even in Ireland, not to mind Cork. You go up a rickety staircase to a small room, dominated by a massive bar, with a piano in the corner. There sits Brian, on his stool at the bar, as much a lord of his fiefdom as Powerscourt once was. He abhors television, and has thrown out those foolish enough to use a mobile phone. He wants pubs to be the havens, the focus for the community, that they once were. You'll find plenty of talk, music and song at the Hi-B, but no smoking. Ireland, like the good European Community member that it used to be, before the present unpleasantness, was among the first to ban smoking in public places. According to Brian O'Donnell, it has tolled the death knell of the licensing trade. Ireland's pub culture, a solace to the people in their hard times, is dying.

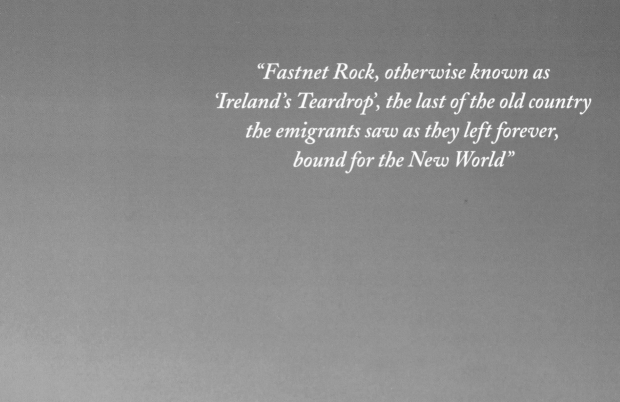

"Fastnet Rock, otherwise known as 'Ireland's Teardrop', the last of the old country the emigrants saw as they left forever, bound for the New World"

BELFAST

DUBLIN

CORK

Clear Island

Cork to Clear Island

Now, we're heading west, over the lovely estuary to the River Bandon, and on past the fishing port, tourist town and gastronomic temple that is Kinsale. More like an English harbour town, it was here that a battle was fought in 1601, which some hold was the beginning of the end for 'Gaelic' Ireland. In that year, an expeditionary force of Spaniards landed here unopposed, to free Ireland from Queen Elizabeth's Protestant thrall. It would have been a great coup for Philip of Spain, but unfortunately the Ulster chieftains, O'Neill and O'Donnell, never got to Kinsale to join their allies, having been put to flight by an English force under Mountjoy. The rebellious earls fled the country, and Ulster, Northern Ireland, was subjugated.

My own memories of Kinsale are of presenting a feature on

The pretty fishing village of Kinsale, where I caught my first and only shark and where, in 1601, the rebellious Irish suffered a crucial defeat

The grotto at Ballinspittle, still a place of prayer and devotion for many Irish Catholics

the place for Irish television, when we were both in our infancy. I actually caught a shark, but it's not recorded for posterity. The cameraman, no sailor, was throwing up on the other side of the boat at the moment of my fishing triumph. Like the Da's, my fishing successes remain, sadly, unsung.

In Holy Catholic Ireland, roadside statues of the Virgin Mary are as familiar as bus shelters and corner shops, yet between 1985 and 1987, such a statue, in the village of Ballinspittle, County Cork, became the cynosure of the world's eyes. For, in July 1985, a small group of locals saw the statue of the Virgin move. The word spread like wildfire through a country dominated by Catholicism. Within a month, BBC camera crews were recording that more than a quarter of a million people had flocked to Ballinspittle to pray to the moving Madonna. Human nature being what it is, statues all over the country were soon on the move. With their usual mixture of sentimentality, piety and cynicism, the Irish saw the funny side. It was claimed that the statue of Master McGrath, the legendary Irish champion greyhound, had been arrested in Kildare for chasing sheep. Another tale had a statue of the Virgin being knocked down by a lorry in Mountmellick as she tried to cross the road.

Yet, I talked to eminently sensible local people who were there on that momentous day in July 1985, and for whom the miracle is still as real as though it happened yesterday. Pat Bowen and Sean

Murray still pray to the statue, but Sean was the local policeman at the time, a man not too easily deceived. Watching the crowd of about four hundred, he saw them gasp in unison, and when he looked at the statue, it seemed to be floating, free of the grotto. So convinced was he that the whole thing was a hoax, that he climbed up early the following morning, expecting to find some kind of trickery. Nothing. He shook the statue, but it was solidly set into the rock.

I met Tim Ryan, a local newspaper reporter at the time, in Ballinspittle village. His estimate was that three out of five people who came to see the moving statue believed that they saw something happen. He himself never believed that it was more than an optical illusion, but indicative of the bad times Ireland was going through: the economy was failing and, for the farmers, it was a catastrophically bad summer, with hay rotting in the fields. Tim thinks that the moving Virgin Mary of Ballinspittle was a desperate reaching out for help from the supernatural. Believers think it was a sign from above that God and His Mother had not forgotten Ireland.

Surging relentlessly on towards the wild Atlantic foam, we find ourselves in West Cork, a popular spot for British residents. Many's the ex-pat who has settled in Skibbereen, Schull and Baltimore for an easier way of life, in easy-going company. A charming little hotel in Baltimore gives me an early morning

Pat Bowen and Sean Murray, who have never doubted the visitation of the Virgin

view from my bedroom of the small harbour and, further out, the wonderfully named Roaring Water Bay. Our boatman, Mícheál, comes to collect us in the harbour from his home on Clear Island. He's taking us out, over the bay, to the great lighthouse of Fastnet Rock, but first he insists that we divert to Clear Island, because he has forgotten the tea.

Through a mercifully calm Atlantic, still as a mill pond, we head for the island, where, sure enough, Mícheál's missus is waiting with the necessary. Sailing on, past a hundred rocks with a thousand seabirds of every shape and size, gulls, guillemots, gannets, soon it looms on the horizon, the great lighthouse, Fastnet, on Ireland's southernmost tip. Mícheál makes his ceremonial pot of tea, and we drink the welcome brew, as the boat wallows gently underneath Fastnet's looming, almost threatening shadow. Fifty metres above sea level, the tallest lighthouse in these islands, yet in 1985, such can be the savagery of the Atlantic, a rogue wave as high as the building itself crashed into it – and every one of the two thousand-odd Cornish granite blocks remained in place. The light is now controlled electronically, but in days of yore, it was manned and the keepers could find themselves stranded for weeks on end, until the Atlantic storms were spent. Yachtsmen have lost

The wild Atlantic was as calm as a mill pond as we braved Roaring Water Bay on our voyage to Clear Island and Fastnet Rock

The little harbour on Clear Island – beautiful, idyllic, a truly peaceful haven

their lives here, in this unpredictable sea, for this is where the gentle land of Ireland ends and the fierce Atlantic begins. They call the Fastnet 'Ireland's Teardrop', because it was the last piece of the old country seen by the emigrants making their way to a new life, in the New World. Sadly, too, the last land seen by the passengers of the *Titanic*, as they sailed to their doom.

Mícheál turns the boat for home, Clear Island. The little harbour welcomes us to an idyllic place, an island of gentle hills and 'boreens', small lanes, fringed with honeysuckle and fuchsia. The western fringes of Ireland are where the native tongue, Gaelic, or Irish, still thrives. Gaelic is the main language on Clear Island, a favourite place for youngsters from all over the country to brush up on their mother tongue. Gaelic is a compulsory subject in all Irish schools; indeed, when I was a lad, if you didn't pass Gaelic you'd failed the whole exam. I think this draconian attitude of government education policy was the reason why Gaelic never caught the imagination or affection of the Irish public, and the language was regarded as useful only if you wanted a job in the Irish Civil Service.

Of course, lip service was paid to the language – mainly on road and street signs, and on Irish radio, but in the sixties, Gaelic was on its last legs. It's a bit different nowadays, with over one and a half million claiming to speak the language. And whether the young people are here for fun, companionship, or what they call 'the craic', they're keeping a flame of national identity alive. Jim was the local bus driver, a Dublin man who came to Clear Island with only a schoolboy's smattering of Gaelic but now speaks it like a native. Which, of course, he is. Not of the island, few are. One hundred and thirty people live here all the year round, swelling to three or four hundred in the summer season.

There's a little restaurant by the harbour, but there are no shops, and no doctor. Everything comes and goes by boat, but when you're standing on a hill on Clear Island, looking over the few cottages and the green fields to the shimmering Atlantic and the Fastnet in the distance, it can seem the most perfect spot on Earth. I asked the bus driver, Jim, if there was any chance that it could be a tax haven, like the Isle of Man. He said you could certainly save money – there was nowhere to spend it.

The boys, girls and staff of the Irish College on Clear Island, the place where youngsters come to brush up on their Gaelic

Back on Mícheál's boat, to Baltimore. On the way, he tells me the bizarre, but true, tale of a Barbary pirate raid on the little port, several centuries ago. Piracy has made a bit of a comeback lately, with ships and sailors being held to ransom for millions by Somali hijackers, but had declined somewhat since the glory days of privateering by the likes of Drake and Blackbeard. Lost in the mists of time have been those scourges of the sea, the pirates of old Barbary. They haven't been forgotten around Baltimore, though. On one terrible day, the pirate ships swept around Roaring Water Bay, and into Baltimore. When they left, they took up to two hundred of the town's inhabitants with them. Whether killed, drowned or sold into slavery in the markets of North Africa, not one of those unfortunate people ever returned to Baltimore.

"Wild and untamed, the Beara Peninsula and a typically winding road through its rugged landscape"

Clear Island to Killarney

And so, it's 'slán leat', goodbye to the rebel county of Cork, and seeing as, if we head further west, we'll be up to our armpits in water, the trusty Dave turns the wheel northwards, toward Kerry...

Kerry, beautiful Kerry – lakes and fells, rivers and mountains, gem in the diadem that is Ireland's scenery. And the greatest gem of all, the very Koh-i-Noor, Killarney. Even in Victorian times, Killarney was a favourite tourist venue for adventurous Brits. They took the train to Holyhead, then the mail boat, and then train again, from Dun Laoghaire to Killarney. And you complain about delays at Terminal 5. Things went a bit quiet for a while, what with two world wars, and a war of independence in Ireland, but around about the sixties, creative folk at Bord Fáilte, the

As the Da used to say, 'Give the Woman in the Bed More Porter'!

newly created Irish Tourist Board, thought about making a few quid by reviving the idea of the country as a holiday destination. The Emerald Isle, Ireland of the Welcomes, Céad Míle Fáilte! It worked, and nowhere more so than in Killarney.

Unfortunately, the town itself has paid the penalty, in commercialisation. It must have been pretty once, on the shores of beautiful lakes and blue mountains, but now it has tacky fast-food shops, and gimcrack souvenirs, and several hotels and bars too many. Step outside the town and it's a different story. There are lovely hotels that almost match the scenery, and the Ring of Kerry. Everybody who comes to Killarney *has* to travel the Ring of Kerry, it's an unwritten rule. It's a one hundred and eighty kilometre round trip that takes you over mountain and by lake to the sea, and back again. And don't bother with 'weather permitting'. Nobody comes to Ireland for the sunshine.

It was what the Irish call 'a soft day' when we set off to tour the Ring. Dave the driver put it bluntly: 'You know, you do this drive on a beautiful day, and you think, this is magnificent. You do it on a day like this…' I asked him if it was difficult to drive, given the distractions of the scenery. 'It might be,' he tersely replied, 'if I could see it…' Because of the weight of tourist traffic on the Ring

Nobody comes to Ireland for the sunshine…

Travelling the Ring of Kerry is an unwritten rule: a few miles west of Killarney is the spectacular Gap of Dunloe…you might even be lucky enough to get weather like this!

road, the county council advise travel in only one direction – anti-clockwise. We're travelling clockwise, and when the tenth large bus had forced us once again into the ditch, I asked, plaintively, 'Is this dangerous, going the wrong way?' His only consolation, he said, was that he would be taking me with him.

I have other memories of Killarney: too long ago to remember the exact year but Ireland had won the Eurovision Song Contest yet again. And let us not forget, even in these days when the Irish entry barely qualifies for the final, that Ireland has won the Eurovision more times than any other country, indeed, three years in succession in the glory days. It must have been one of them when myself and the BBC TV team (do three people constitute a team?) found ourselves in the Great Southern Hotel, Killarney, our base for the great event, which, for reasons never fully explained, was to be held in an equestrian centre in Millstreet, County Cork – a village without so much as a boarding house to its name. He was

some salesman, that equestrian centre owner from the middle of nowhere. For he sold the idea not only to Irish television but to the European Broadcasting Union.

There's more: he boldly suggested that the inhabitants of Millstreet might do well to smarten up the place, in view of the coming influx of foreigners from all over Europe. Paint the houses, tidy up the gardens, sweep the main street, so that the village might reflect well on them, and on him. There was general agreement but, of course, there's always a begrudger. This one

There it stands, shrouded as ever in lowering clouds, proud Carrantuohill, Ireland's loftiest peak

was be-damned if he was going to paint his house for any Johnny foreigner. Hadn't his forefathers fought and died for freedom? A raffle was organised by our entrepreneur. The prize was a weekend, all expenses paid, in a lavish Dublin hotel. And, as luck would have it, the recalcitrant villager won the raffle! Off he popped to Dublin, and do you know, when he returned to Millstreet, some good fairy had painted his house and tidied up his garden for him. No wonder some people still believe in the 'little folk'.

Although, as with nearly all of the Song Contests I commentated upon, I have absolutely no recollection of a single song, I can certainly remember the journey on the Big Night from Killarney to Millstreet. For Michael Devine, a great man who always chauffeured me around whenever I visited for the Eurosong, not only drove me the twenty miles on the winding country lanes, but organised a police motorcycle escort! He did it again, in Dublin, after yet another Irish win. Have you any idea the feeling of power and grandeur it bestows on even a modest head, such as my own, to have a police escort stopping the traffic for you? Racing through red lights, ignoring 'stop' signs, to the whine of police sirens? Master of the Universe! We roared up to the Point, the huge arena in Dublin, something of a contrast to the Millstreet experience, and the motorcycle escort sped off to collect the Irish president, who was coming to the Song Contest a little later. Only in Ireland...

The Skelligs

Ireland is an island – 'Thank God we're surrounded by water,' as the writer Dominic Behan put it so well – and the Aran Islands are not the only pieces of Erin's Isle that find themselves offshore, fending for themselves. Helen and I had a holiday in the lovely little town of Kenmare some years ago, and explored both sides of the beautiful Kenmare River; each remarkable, a feast to the eye. The Beara Peninsula has a subtropical garden, with all manner of exotic plants and trees from the world's rainforests, planted centuries ago by an Englishman who settled there, a doctor, it's said, from Cromwell's conquering army.

On the other side of the river, a road that winds through a landscape that should belong to the Scottish Highlands and carries you to the seaside town of Waterville, home of another great golf course, and a place where Charlie Chaplin used to holiday, far from the madding crowd. On the way, a sight to make you stop the car, get off your bike or pause in your

Extraordinary that men should cut themselves off from the rest of the world to live in such hardship in the name of God

The Skellig Rocks – like
two grey ghosts rising
out of the Atlantic

rambling: there, stark against the skyline, pounded endlessly by the Atlantic, the Skelligs – Great Skellig and Skellig Michael.

Skellig Michael is cone-shaped, rising like a rocket to seven hundred feet. There's a small mooring, and a thousand steep steps carry you to an extraordinary sight: a tenth-century monastic settlement of two churches, two oratories and several beehive-shaped 'clochans', cells where the monks lived, and prayed, their lives a constant storming of Heaven in prayer on behalf of their fellow men. How they survived, not to mind lived, is impossible to imagine. No longer, of course, and they tell me that, although the occasional film crew seem to gain access, the rock is now closed to the public and any monks that may seek solitude there. The Skelligs are left to the birds.

"The Ring of Kerry route runs past Portmagee, a fishing village across the water from Valentia Island and a great place for the craic"

Killarney to Valentia Island

I'm getting bedsores sitting in Dave's car, as we head relentlessly off again, to Valentia Island, where the first coaxial cable was laid between Europe and America, changing communications forever, allowing both sides of the Atlantic to be in constant touch for the first time. This important place became a community, with accommodation for the engineers, technicians and their families, with facilities, such as a tennis court, which far exceeded the grasp of any other small community in the area. The grand buildings are still there, well preserved, as indeed are the houses, many of which are still inhabited, mostly by holidaymakers. I didn't see anyone play tennis, though. Well, it was raining.

Valentia is an island, so you have to take a ferry, or cross the bridge, to the mainland and the little harbour at Portmagee. We

The little harbour at Portmagee with its brightly painted houses

stayed the night there, in the delightful Bridge Inn. Fresh fish for dinner, and I woke the following morning, as I had in Baltimore, to a view of wheeling gulls and little boats. The night before, the Bridge Inn, whose proprietor has a pleasing baritone himself, was packed to the gunwales for a musical soirée. The Irish call it 'the craic'. Now, I'll be honest and straight with you: I'm not big on 'singing pubs'. I'm an urban Irishman, a 'gurrier', as they say in Dublin. If somebody starts up with a banjo or a bodhrán (a small drum) near me, I throw some change in his hat and move along the bar. Why people can't sit quietly and have a conversation over a pint of stout, without someone letting fly with an accordion or some old come-all-ye, is beyond me. And, despite what every Englishman thinks of the Irish, I've never been on a horse in my life.

Anyway, despite curmudgeons like myself, the Irish love 'the craic'. It's Gaelic for 'fun', and I have to admit, on that evening of music, dance and song at the Bridge Inn, the craic lived up to its name. Little girls, who could have walked straight into the cast of *Riverdance*, delighted us with jigs and reels, the fiddlers kept the music going, and the songs – ah, the songs. It's always been a source of mystery to me why Irish musicians, particularly fiddlers, with all the merry singing and dancing going on around them, look as if they're playing at a funeral. The atmosphere is one of unbounded good-natured cheer, despite most of the songs being along the well-known Irish theme of dying, or leaving, never to return.

You can't throw a stone in Riga, Kiev or Vladivostok without hitting an 'Irish' pub. The pub is Ireland's greatest export, but I guarantee that you won't find many Irish men or women in them. It's enough that we've had to export so many people.

What would Irish music-making be without the pint of stout? Don't tell me that's a glass of orange juice…

Dingle Bay

It could never be said that Wogan family holidays ranged the length and breadth of the country, relying, as they did, on the Da meeting somebody on the other side of the bacon slicer and taking their recommendations. I hate to say it, but the Da was not a particularly good judge of his fellow men, always making the assumption that everybody was as honest as him and, indeed, shared his standards. It would explain the dingy boarding houses of Galway, Ballybunion and Courtown Harbour, but could scarcely excuse the dreadful house in the wilds of Kerry that Michael Wogan brought his unfortunate family to, one summer holiday long ago.

We've already established, beyond reasonable doubt, the beauties of the county of Kerry. And, indeed, the spot on which the Da landed us was no also-ran in the scenery stakes, down on Dingle Bay, overlooking the spectacular strand of Inch. Inch Strand, incidentally, was where David Lean shot the spectacular film *Ryan's Daughter*. They still talk, the old actors in Neary's pub in Dublin, of those great days when Mr Lean kept half of Irish Equity in employment for months on end, while he awaited a suitable sunset on Inch Strand. It never came to pass, and eventually David Lean flew his crew to a beach in South Africa, where a fellow could be sure of a decent sunset.

It could hardly be said that Wogan family holidays were luxurious affairs but we seldom lacked for scenery

Inch Strand – the very beach where director David Lean waited for a sunset that, unfortunately, never came…

The house the Da, trusting as ever, rented unseen, while scarcely beautiful and lacking anywhere comfortable to sit, had one other pretty serious drawback: any water had to be drawn from a well. Of water closets there were none. God knows what the Ma had to say, but the Brother and I are pictured having a high old time on a donkey, and I'm sure there were hens and chickens. The house belonged to a lovely, lonely woman called Mary-Ann, and her silent husband, about twice her age, whose name we never heard. Mary-Ann took us on the donkey and cart to the local village, Annascaul. I fell off the cart, and had a lump the size of a duck egg on my forehead for the remainder of the holiday. Looking back, that all must have happened in about 1948 or so, but it could just as easily have been 1848, or a hundred years before that.

"*With the mountain of Mullaghanattin and its horseshoe ridge in the background, a road snakes through the spectacular Kerry countryside*"

Valentia Island to Tralee

Onwards then, and upwards to proud County Kerry's capital, Tralee. The town is famous for more than that – there's the world-famous song, 'The Rose of Tralee', which begat Ireland's most-viewed television programme, *The Rose of Tralee* beauty contest. Except, of course, as any committee member will tell you, it's not a 'beauty contest'.

Pursuant to the words of the song Count John McCormack made famous – 'Yet 'twas not her beauty alone that won me' – the Rose must have much more to her than just good looks. Intelligence, a ready grasp of world affairs, a pleasing personality and, if at all possible, familiarity with a musical instrument do not come amiss. And bikinis are out. I've never understood why beauty contests the world over, from Miss Universe, to Miss

'By Killarney's Lakes and Fells', as the old song puts it so well

World, to Miss USA, to the Rose herself, seek to perpetuate the ridiculous idea that a 'beauty contest' is not about looks.

Way back in the fifties, Ireland was becoming aware of its potential as a tourist attraction, and Tralee wasn't going to be left behind the gravy train. In her charming little house in the town, I met the woman who helped create 'The Rose', and became its first lady president, Margaret Dwyer, whose Brooklyn accent, even after fifty-odd years, still hasn't left her. Initially the aim was modest enough: bring Ireland to Tralee – but by the late sixties, it had become an international event. Irish expatriate centres from all over the world were sending their 'Roses' to Tralee. Irish television began to cover the pageant, and since I was one of the new boys on the box, and had even made my way to the BBC, they invited me to compère the event. I remember being impressed with the number of girls from far-flung foreign fields – Paraguay, for instance. I can recall thinking that the competition among girls of Irish descent can't have been that intense in Asunción.

I presented *The Rose* from 1968 to 1970, and in the last year, before they found somebody who would do the job properly, I brought Helen with me, to savour the delights of Tralee, en fête. One afternoon, we were invited to the Festival Club, where the elite could intermingle, without some eejit throwing a pint of stout all over them. There was music, and dancing to Noel Healy and his Cordovox, an instrument that combined the accordion and the melodeon to the best advantage. I've never seen one since, not even at the Eurovision Song Contest. A young Kerry blade approached Helen: 'Would you like to dance?'

Now, in the Ireland of my young manhood, and, probably, in Kerry even to this day, when a fellow asked a girl to dance, a refusal not only offended, it was simply not done. It mattered not if your man was drunk as a skunk, smelt to high heaven, or was eighty years of age, no decent girl ever turned a man down for a dance – the slight on his manhood would be too grievous. The missus, never one to pay homage to the fragile self-esteem of the Irish male, said: 'No, thank you, I'm talking to my friends.' He was affronted, astounded by the rejection, but, recovering, he assuaged his proud Kerry manhood: 'Ah well,' he said, 'you're too old for me anyway.'

The thorn among the Roses...

The marvellous Margaret Dwyer, the real 'Rose of Tralee'

Lovely Cathy Quinn, Rose of '69, who has kept all the incriminating evidence

I did not see the Rose contest on our whistle-stop tour, it was on too late in the year, but in Dublin, later on in our filming, I met up with the still beautiful Cathy Quinn, the Rose of 1969. A green-eyed student nurse from Longford, she was the Dublin Rose, and remembers clearly the great night in Tralee. She'd kept the programme and the pictures, and the ones in the paper that showed her back on duty as a night-nurse in a Dublin hospital, a couple of nights later. A far, fierce hour and sweet indeed. Cathy married a surgeon named Murphy, whom I played rugby against in school, and whose father was a pal of mine from the Irish police Special Branch, who sat outside the studio with a Smith & Wesson revolver in his pocket, while I read the news on Radio Éireann.

Who's the eejit with the sideburns?

"The edge of The Burren, meaning 'great rock' – a remarkable limestone plateau, one of the largest such landscapes in Europe"

Tralee
to Limerick

Small world... but as I've said before, a big little island, and after seven hundred kilometres on the road, we're coming into the place where I was born; I'm coming home to the City of the Broken Treaty, where perfidious Albion did the dirty yet again on our brave boys – Limerick, on the mighty Shannon, the longest river in these islands, running from here all the way up to the lakes of Northern Ireland. As I sat in my hotel room, I looked out at the great river, and the swans sheltering from the rain under Sarsfield Bridge, named for the hero of the Siege of Limerick in the Williamite wars. They might have coupled it with my name, I crossed that bridge so often. Four times a day, back and forth to Crescent College, little legs pumping like a steam engine. I've always associated my cycling with that of 'The Third Policeman'

The imposing Gothic-style chuch of St Munchin's, Limerick, overlooking the banks of the mighty Shannon

in Flann O'Brien's great book, who did so much of it that he became half-man, half-bicycle. A couple of years ago, the mayor and city council of Limerick graciously conferred on me the honour of Freeman of the City, and now I can drive a herd of sheep or cattle over Sarsfield Bridge, as the mood takes me.

The Da was from Wicklow, and the Ma had lived in Dublin all her life, so coming to a provincial backwater was a shock to their systems. Still, the Da had been offered the managership of the Limerick branch of Leverett & Frye, and without the extra money they couldn't have afforded to marry. So, Limerick it was. The Da, happy as Larry to be married to the woman he'd always loved, and devoted, with almost as much intensity, to his job, settled immediately. Rose Wogan accepted her lot stoically, but never really left Dublin. Every summer she'd go back to her mother, the beloved 'Muds', and her sisters, my maiden aunts, for a couple of months. Every Christmas and Easter, for a couple of weeks.

Back in Limerick, Michael Wogan took great pleasure in catering for the landed gentry, the horse people, the relics of old decency, the remittance men of the counties of Limerick and Tipperary who frequented his shop for the delights that they had left behind in London, Cheltenham and the Shires. Exotic fruits, poppadums, terrines, preservatives, French cheeses, and, of course, Limerick ham, of which there is none finer in the known world.

The Brother, Brian, went to the trouble of taking the train all the way from Dublin to meet me at Limerick station, so that we could the better relive our young lives in 18, Elm Park, Ennis Road, and the delights of the Da's grocery shop. It was a relief to find that they were both where we left them. Leverett & Frye is now a clothing store, but Brian and I had little trouble recollecting where the cash desk used to be located, and the cheese counter, and where the Da sliced the ham, with the meticulous care that he brought to everything he did.

Before Brian was born, six and a half years later than me, the Da would take me out, having fitted a little saddle on the crossbar of his bike, to fish on the banks of the Maigue, a tributary of the Shannon. It took the best part of an hour, through the town and out past the docks, and then the cement works. Along with the

ABOVE: *The Ma and I take to the boulevards of Limerick*

ABOVE RIGHT: *Holy Communion day at Elm Park, Limerick. That's me on the left, with next-door neighbour Sean Cleary. Those were not false ears...*

factory where they made Cleeve's Toffee and Ranks flour mill, these were the few places where men could find work in those days. And the Craven 'A' cigarette factory. The docks and the flour mill are still there; I'm not sure about the cement works but the toffee and the fags are long gone.

Sunday was the only day the Da didn't work, so that was the day we went fishing. Rod and tackle, flask of tea and packet of corned-beef sandwiches stowed at the back, and look out trout and flounder! Actually, on the muddy Maigue what he caught mostly was eel, a delicacy nowadays but something you threw back into the river then. Not that the Ma would have touched it with a bargepole anyway, not to mind cook the thing. Sometimes the Da would try another little river, where the mayfly danced and the corncrake sang its strange song, and there he would elegantly cast his line for trout. They didn't give themselves up as easily as eels or flounders, but the Da was a real fisherman – it wasn't the catch that mattered, it was the skill of the cast, the preparation of the flies that would snare the fish. Often, it would be hours before the first cast was made. I frequently think that my inability to prepare, my impatience, my desire to get going, to make things up as I go along, are a direct result of watching my father get ready to fish.

Every other Sunday, we'd take the long walk across town to the Markets Field, where Limerick Football Club gave their all in the League of Ireland, and for that again, off we'd go in the opposite direction to the Gaelic Games field, to watch the hurling.

Limerick is, and ever was, a sporting city. On the main street, O'Connell Street, is a statue of two rugby players, which speaks volumes about Limerick's major sporting obsession. For this is the very heartland of Irish rugby. Unlike the rest of the country, and very similar to Welsh towns, everybody in Limerick plays rugby. Docker, labourer, banker, solicitor all scrum down together. It's no wonder that some of Ireland's great clubs and greatest rugby players hail from here. In the suburbs is Thomond Park, where the provincial side, Munster, play, heroes and winners of Europe's Heineken Cup. I'm proud to say that I played as a lad on the sacred turf, but the new Thomond is a far cry from the concrete changing rooms I remember. Now a magnificent stadium, proudly bearing the legend, 'Irish by birth. Munster by the grace of God.'

Limerick has changed a great deal since I left, as it should, in nearly sixty years, but 18, Elm Park, Ennis Road is still as Brian and I remember it. Little garden in the front, an arch over the front door, but inside much smaller than we thought. Well, it would be – we were much smaller. Changed inside, as well: the new owner, who kindly invited the Brother and myself in, has caused what used to be the 'good' room, where nobody sat unless the priest or the doctor was visiting, to flow into the dining room, a great improvement. He has extended the kitchen as well, out into the back yard. Good to see the side wall, which the Da built up to avoid prying eyes, still standing. He'd be proud. And I swear I can still hear the echo of his fine baritone, as we look into the old bathroom. Every evening, before bed, he would shave, in

ABOVE LEFT: *The Brother, Brian, who took the train from Dublin to join me in Limerick to look over the Da's old grocery store in O'Connell Street*

ABOVE: *The two of us outside 18, Elm Park, Ennis Road, Limerick*

preparation for the next day, and as he shaved cause all of little Elm Park to ring to the strains of 'The Floral Dance', 'Valentine's Goodbye' from *Faust* and 'Dead for Bread'. The last was far from being a favourite of my mother's, who could often be heard to complain, 'For God's sake, Michael, sing something cheerful!'

Every week, my dear godmother, Auntie May, who was the manager of a bookshop in Dublin, would send Brian and me a parcel of new comics and books that became our window on a world outside of a small Irish town. Just as the BBC Light Programme did with *Dick Barton – Special Agent*, *Take It From Here* and *The Goons*. I've never forgiven the BBC for giving dear old Dick the elbow and then, ultimately, replacing him with an 'everyday story of country folk' – *The Archers*. I've played my part on at least three episodes of *The Archers*, but what wouldn't I have given to be at the shoulder of Dick, Jock and Snowy in some perilous adventure. I suppose it could be said that listening to the BBC instead of Irish radio turned me into a proper little West Brit, but perhaps it prepared me for what life was to bring me later.

As I grew toward adolescence, I made a great discovery: Subbuteo. Table football. In no time I had converted my pals, and for two glorious years we travelled back and forward to each other's houses, home and away, for closely fought encounters between our teams of tiny footballers. We had a league, a cup competition, friendlies too, all with our English league teams: Arsenal, Wolves, Blackpool (mine – I was a Stanley Matthews man) and the rest. Myself and the boys – Billy, James, John

Crescent College, where you could say it all started. I made my debut as a public speaker there, in the school debates

Jim Sexton, Bobby Mulrooney and Mick Leahy join me in the hall of Crescent College, where once we danced with the girls of the Laurel Hill Convent

– recall those palmy, innocent days, whenever we meet. My loyal friends turned up for my inauguration as a Freeman of Limerick, and there, waiting to greet me outside our old school, Crescent College, is dear James, with Bobby and Mick. I don't hold it against Mick that, on another occasion, he told a tale of my prowess on the rugby field: 'Wogan was a prop forward, but for some reason, found himself the last line of defence, as our opponents broke through. Their huge centre, ball in hand, surged for our tryline. Only Wogan stood in his way. Wogan had two alternatives: crash tackle the monster, or stand aside. Wogan stood aside. It's been suggested that he whispered, "And good luck with the conversion" as his opponent swept by.'

Crescent College is a tutorial school now; the Jesuit fathers, who brought us enlightenment, education, religion and the occasional sore pair of hands from a leather strap, have gone, the church next door, where I was an altar boy and chorister, closed. How the memories crowded back as we walked the old corridors, peered into the old classrooms and remembered the teachers, some with affection, others, as we recalled the fear they generated, with something less. We entered the hall, newly built when I was a pupil, used for exams, concerts and dances. Ah, the dances. In an extraordinary burst of enlightenment, the Jesuits and the nuns who ran the girls' school decided to have dances a couple of times a year. Boys and girls together, mixing, touching. It was revolutionary for Holy Catholic Ireland! It wasn't as free and easy as all that, of course. The nuns and priests moved among us as

Thomond Bridge over the Shannon and King John's Castle, part of Limerick's medieval heritage

we danced; there wasn't a lot of what you could call bodily contact. The Crescent hall was where I first spoke publicly, at school debates, so I suppose you might think the place has a lot to answer for...

When I was fifteen, Michael Wogan's great success as Manager, Limerick branch of Leverett & Frye, was rewarded with promotion to General Manager, Leverett & Frye. It not only changed the life of the family, it was the crucial change of my whole life. If I had stayed in Limerick, what would have been my future? A bank in Limerick? University in Dublin? Would I have ever applied to Irish radio for a job? And so, the Wogans moved on, to Dublin's fair city.

My caravan has rested long enough in my home city – we must away, past Clare, and its sweeping panoramas of the Cliffs of Moher (known to American tourists as 'The Cliffs of Mohair') and the remarkable limestone plateau of The Burren. Our great friend, the late Gordon Wood, Irish rugby international and British Lion, and father of Keith, Irish rugby captain and British

Lion, had that rara avis in the Limerick of the fifties, a motor car. He would take us down to Quilty, on the Clare coast, with its thundering Atlantic surf, into which he and the Da would hurl optimistic lines baited with the lugworm that I helped dig up on the beach (in between the worm-hole and its little mound of sand, in case you were thinking of having a go yourself) in the hopes of catching a naïve bass or flounder. The Ma would sit patiently by the Thermos, the sandwiches and buns, while Brian and I threw ourselves down precipitous sand dunes. The sun always shone. They say that your memories of childhood days are ever sunny, and I suppose Limerick's rain is the exception that proves the rule.

I have many happy memories, too, of the hospitality of the Clancy family, who had a house shrewdly positioned between Lahinch's two great golf courses. I can't pretend the weather was always benign there, either, although you always know what to expect on Lahinch golf course – all you have to do is keep a weather-eye on the goats that crop the fairways. If they're shelter-ing under the eaves of the clubhouse, put away your putting iron and ribbed-faced mashie niblick, and head for the comforts of the bar. If the goats are out there, keeping the rough almost playable, tee up and give it your best shot, although even on what the mem-bers would call 'a fine day', you'll be picking the sand out of your

Bunratty Castle, County Clare – a Norman keep where you can now eat, drink and be merry to the sound of harp and melodious Irish voices. And you can also down a pint in Durty Nelly's nearby

teeth and playing into a wind that a friend of mine once graphically described as 'strong enough to blow a tinker off his missus'.

The Clancys didn't stint on breakfast any more than they did on kindness and generosity, and I remember one morning, after partaking of bacon, eggs, black pudding, fried bread and soda bread with marmalade, washed down with copious draughts of tea, marching into the teeth of the wind up the first at Lahinch, and saying to mine host, the wonderful Michael Clancy, 'I don't know if I can make this, after all that food.' He looked at me pityingly. 'Lahinch,' he said, magisterially, 'is no place to be playing hungry golf...'

Lahinch Golf Club, like the equally punishingly magnificent Doonbeg course, just along the coast, does not make it easy for the high-handicapper such as myself. Apart from natural hazards such as the wind, the rain and the rough, it's rare enough to be able to see the green you're supposed to be hitting to, from the tee. The eagle-eyed can pick out little white stones clinging to the sides of huge sand dunes, which are supposed to give you an idea of the general direction in which you should be hitting the ball, if you ever hope to see the pin and the green. As I've said before, 'journey' is a debased word these days, but I never stand on the tee at Lahinch or Doonbeg without a hollow feeling that I'm starting on a journey that might not only have an unhappy ending, but might never end...

They tell a tale in Lahinch of an American visitor, eager to pit his golfing prowess against the great links, hitting to a short par three, guarded by sand hills that make the green and its flag invisible. He hit what he felt was a good one, straight over the little white stone high upon the hill. To his delight, when he finally got to the green, the caddy was all smiles – 'Good man, sir! A hole in one!' When he had calmed himself over a triumph that he would recount to all who would listen at Akron, Ohio, Golf and Country Club, the American pressed a hundred dollars on his protesting caddy. It is said that after this remarkable occurrence, visiting golfers had holes-in-one with increasing frequency until the Greens Committee got wind of the scam. The scandal was smartly suppressed. Sometimes, the golf rules of the Royal and Ancient just spoil the fun.

Aran Islands

Why do they always have to dig out pictures you'd rather forget?

In my day, Carty's *Irish History* ignored the realities of the twentieth century and spent much of its erudition on saga and mythology. According to Carty, the first people to take over the place were the Fomorians, a rough crowd led by a hooligan known as Balor of the Evil Eye, who could shrivel an Irish elk with a passing glance. The Giant's Causeway in County Antrim was the Fomorians' 'stairway', apparently, but this has been contradicted in the sagas of Finn McCool, which state categorically that he threw the causeway there in a fit of pique.

Then there came the Partholonians, followed closely by the Nemedians and, every schoolboy's favourites, the Fir Bolgs. 'Fir Bolg' means 'Bag Man' in English, and they got their name because they were descended from the unfortunate slaves who carried the bagfuls of bricks that built the Pyramids. I kid you not – we were actually taught this stuff as if it was fact. Anyway, our beloved Fir Bolgs were only there for a couple of millennia before they got it in the neck from the Tuatha Dé Danann, who cheated, with magic as well as a doughty battler known as Lugh of the Long Arm.

It was said, with conviction, that the Fir Bolgs' last stand was at Dun Aengus, a Neolithic rampart, the ruins of which can still be seen on Inishmore, the largest of the three Aran Islands, which lie off the coast of County Galway. It's a mythological footnote, but the Tuatha Dé Danann got the elbow in their turn from a crowd called the Milesians. Not the Salesians, mind. They were the kindly nuns who first taught me manners in Ferrybank, Limerick. It appears that the Milesians were a cultured bunch, for a change, and had a poet, who travelled northwards, and a harpist, who went in a southerly direction. And to this day, children, Ireland's poets all come from Northern Ireland, and its singers from the south. Where this leaves Van Morrison has yet to be discussed.

The Aran Islands have long been regarded as the last bastion of true Gaelic culture, the ultimate Celtic Fringe. On the

islands, the way of life has hardly changed for hundreds of years. The hardy inhabitants still brave the Atlantic waves in simple wooden boats known as 'currachs', although their lot has been eased by tourism, and the cottage industry that has produced the famous Aran sweater. (I once modelled an Aran sweater in an Irish magazine. The caption read: 'Terry Wogan, RTE's gay bachelor compère.')

Talking of myths, some numpty of a historian had the immortal gall to suggest that the inhabitants of the Aran Islands were not actually the lost Gaels, the last of the Celts, but the descendants of English soldiers, a garrison quartered there by none other than the hated Cromwell! Holds about as much water as those bags of bricks…

"*Derryclare Lough and the blue mountains of the Twelve Bens, Galway, where, in the past, I spent many happy days*"

Limerick to Galway

And so it's on to the City of the Tribes – Galway, the romantic capital of the west of Ireland, on the very edge of the Celtic Fringe. Next stop, Manhattan.

Galway is famous for its races, where, legend has it, more money is gambled than at Cheltenham itself. There's the Galway Oyster Festival, where those two partners, Guinness and the bivalved mollusc, mix and mingle to the gourmet's delight. Late for the races, and too early for the oyster, there not being an 'r' in the month when we were there, we did manage to get a passing glimpse of the grand parade of the Galway Arts Festival, a spectacular combination of the Notting Hill Carnival and the Edinburgh Fringe. I have no doubt that I missed half a dozen other festivals in Galway – there must be a Salmon Festival (you

The dramatic Cliffs of Moher. Like the rest of the Clare coast, at the mercy of the thundering Atlantic surf

The grand parade of the Galway Arts Festival, and its inspirational director, Noeline Kavanagh (with me, far left). Galway is the spiritual and real home of Irish festivities. Arts, oysters, horseracing – Galway's got 'em all!

can see the fish swimming up the weir, in the middle of the town), and don't tell me that poetry and music don't have their moments of glory.

I met Noeline Kavanagh, a tall ball of fire who is the artistic director of a theatre company, Macnas. They stage the fantastic parade that's watched by eighty thousand people, weaving its colourful way through Galway's medieval streets. Macnas means 'joyful abandonment', which is, in itself, a commentary on how my country has changed, from the rigidly Roman Catholic inhibitions and restrictions of my boyhood. Even then, Galway always boasted a strong theatrical tradition: the 'Taidhbhearch', which I only hope I've spelt correctly, was a Gaelic-speaking theatre company, based in one of the oldest parts of Galway, the Claddagh. My wife Helen's mother came from further along the coast, Sligo, but the mighty Tim, her larger-than-life father, hailed from Galway, and when Tim and Ellie, Helen's mother, married, he gave her a traditional wedding gift, a Claddagh ring. Helen wears it now, and you can buy them to this day, a simple silver ring of two hands entwined.

Whereas Dublin is 'Stag City Central' for many Brits out to paint themselves and the town red on a lads' weekend, Galway is the jumping joint for the single Irish man or woman who likes to party. It's got the youngest, fastest-growing population in the country, and you won't find them huddled over a turf fire in the evening. The town itself is over a thousand years old – perhaps, in terms of trade, the most international of Ireland's ports. There's an ancient stone wall here by the docks, known as the 'Spanish Arch', recalling the days when this was the country's principal trading centre with Spain and France. They say that the dark-haired, brown-complexioned boys and girls you see in these parts, so unlike the pale-skinned, red-haired, freckled rest of the Irish population, carry the blood of Spanish traders. Well, I did say that this was a romantic place.

Macnas have taken theatre to the streets of Galway but, frankly, I feel that they were leaning against an open door here. We'd hardly got over the excitement of the festival parade than they're ready to execute Charles I. You may well make the salient point that it's been done before, in London in 1649, but Galway has a connection with the regicide, and is not the kind of town to ignore it.

I saw a party of Roundheads, starring Oliver Cromwell – not one of Ireland's favourite Englishmen, since he burned several towns to the ground and left their defenders' heads on spikes – followed by King Charles, complete with flowing locks and a bevy of distraught women protesting his innocence, being dragged along in a most unseemly manner to the place of execution, in this case a pub, for reasons we will shortly understand. Oliver Cromwell announces that the King has shown himself to be an enemy of Parliament, and is sentenced to death. Cromwell calls upon the axeman executioner to do his duty. The royal executioner refuses, overcome by the blandishments of the King's mistresses. Who will do the dirty deed? Up steps a new recruit, only too ready to take the King's head off, which he does, with alacrity. I hope that you were paying attention, because this is where it all becomes clear: the executioner who volunteered to separate the King's head from his body was a Galwayman called Gunning, and the very pub at which this historic scene was enacted, the Kings Head, was his reward from a grateful Cromwell and Parliament.

There's more: Jonathan Gunning, who played the role of executioner with such gusto, is a direct descendant of Richard, who so nefariously gained the Kings Head pub. A role, you must truly say, he was born to play. He did point out that a Gunning wasn't the only one responsible for the King's unfortunate demise. Not only that, Jonathan Gunning produced a copy of the death warrant of Charles I. There are fifty-nine signatories, in 1649. And one of them is a Wogan, Sir Thomas of that ilk. I don't get it – Wogans fought for the Stuarts in the Williamite wars, and here they want the head of one. With all that changing of sides, it's no wonder the great-grandfather ended up bootmaking and roofing in County Wicklow…

My memories of Galway are all of Salthill, the seaside bit of the city, for that's where the little Wogan family went on holiday. Once, but never again. The Da was a man who put great faith in people that was often misplaced, as it certainly was in whoever recommended the boarding house in Salthill which, even after

Getting the old feet wet in Galway Bay. The place also lends its name to a well-known song that has spawned several versions and is particularly popular with Irish emigrants the world over

almost sixty years, I remember as a place that we should have left, on first sight, in a marked manner, for the comfort of home. I think that we were there for only a week, but even from this distance it seemed much longer.

Yet, on the photographic evidence, all seems pretty jolly. There we are, promenading in the sun, the Ma in her floral print, me with the ears, which in a high wind could have carried me out to sea. The Brother sports a pullover that could only have been knitted by a maiden aunt, and then there's the Da, Michael Wogan, victualler to toffs and gentry, with a fag hanging out of the corner of his mouth. And a beret, firm evidence that my father was on holiday. When cycling to work, or going fishing, he wore a cap. Sometimes even a hat, when going to Mass on Sunday morning, but on holiday it was the beret. There's further proof, if proof were needed, in pictures taken on another family holiday, in Ballybunion, County Kerry. As the photographic evidence shows, he would have been better off sticking with a cap. Only a Frenchman with a baguette under his arm and a Gauloises at a rakish angle can carry off a beret.

It wasn't Salthill that was the problem; it was the boarding house. More particularly, the woman running it. The fishing was great, with the mackerel literally flinging themselves at you. The trouble was, when the Da took the catch back, in the hopes that we might have them for tea as a change from the leaf of lettuce, sliced tomato, half a boiled egg and thinly spread butter on bread that was the hostess's idea of a decent meal, we never saw the fish again. What made it worse was the woman's cheery salutation to us as we left the place every day: 'Off ye go now, and work up an appetite for yer tea!'

The present Lady Wogan's family, on her father's side, hail from County Galway; the name is Joyce. It's a name not unknown in the region; in fact, there were so many of the ilk in part of the county at one time that it was known as 'Joyce Country'. I always had a sneaking suspicion that Helen's father thought it was named after him. Galway and Connemara (Gaelic for 'Hound of the Sea') is a hard, unyielding land of rock and barren soil, the embodiment of Cromwell's boast that he was going to drive the Irish across the Shannon, 'to Hell or Connacht'. It was here,

The Wogans on holiday in Salthill. The Da's beret gives the game away...

Croagh Patrick, County Mayo. It was on this mountaintop that St Patrick was inspired to convert the pagan Irish to Christianity

in the west, that the Great Famine struck its most bitter blows, and from here that the greatest number of emigrants took the sad road that led to Liverpool and New York. They say that on a clear day, from Connemara's capital, Clifden, you can see the Statue of Liberty. That's if you ever get a clear day...

In the past, I've had many a happy day in the Twelve Bens, the blue mountains that overshadow Connemara. The great lake, Lough Corrib, has on its shore a grand hotel, Ashford Castle, a former home of the Guinness family, all towers, battlements and crenellations, a marvellous fake castle, along the lines of Windsor, or if you want to be that way, Walt Disney's Magic Kingdom. There's a drawbridge, a golf course and lovely views across the lake, which in turn houses a little island on which, as ever in Ireland, stood an old monastery. The Irish monks liked to keep their distance – not just from marauding Vikings but local chieftains after the church treasures.

Ashford Castle is in the village of Cong, which resembles not so much a typical Irish village as a film set. Whenever you visit there, you feel as if the whole place is dismantled in the evening, and put together in time for the cameras the following morning. It's all the fault of *The Quiet Man*, a popular film of the fifties that starred John Wayne and Maureen O'Hara, he a returned Irish-American boxer, she a flame-haired Irish lovely in a red petticoat. If you're ever lucky enough to stay at Ashford Castle, you can't miss it. They show it permanently, on every television in every room. The film has been a nice little earner for Cong, too. When I was last there, a little local girl conducted a regular guided tour of the place, and the various locations where the film has been shot.

Onwards and upwards brings you to Mayo, site of Croagh Patrick, the mountain on whose summit the patron saint of Ireland vanquished the country's snakes. Many pious people make the difficult climb to the top, often in bare feet, to pay homage and pray. A little further up the coast, in Donegal, is Lough Derg and St Patrick's Purgatory, a place of pilgrimage and penitence for the Irish since the thirteenth century. Throughout the year, in their hundreds, nay thousands, those wishing to be cleansed of their sins are rowed to the island, where they endure three days and nights of prayer, fasting and little sleep, with only hot water and pepper to stave off the hunger pangs. My wife did the Purgatory in her younger days; I'm afraid that I missed out on 'the gift of faith', but Helen has never told me whether she got what she prayed for, or whether St Patrick let her down…

Mayo is also where you will find the town of Bohola, with a couple of hundred inhabitants, and about twenty self-made millionaires in Britain and the States; and Knock, Ireland's answer to Lourdes, with basilica, awful religious souvenir shops and holy water on tap, a tribute to a determined parish priest, who not only did his bit for the greater glory of God, but was instrumental in having an airport built at Knock which has been a boon to this part of Ireland.

There's a little runway at Castlebar as well – I know because I landed there, years ago, in the company of Mr Acker Bilk, who was to provide the musical interlude for the Castlebar International Song Contest, for which I was to be Chairman of the Judges. I well remember the runway because, for an awful moment, I thought our little plane was going to be stopped only by the stout

Lough Corrib, between Galway and Mayo. The second largest lake in Ireland, it's reputed to have over a thousand islands

brick wall at runway's end. I remember little of the song contest, but as we stood in the rain in the car park when it was all over, the promoter shook my hand and handed me a rusty biscuit box containing the sodden notes that were my fee.

In France, a couple of years ago, I met an Englishman called 'Lord Mayo'. I doubt if he'd ever been there in his life.

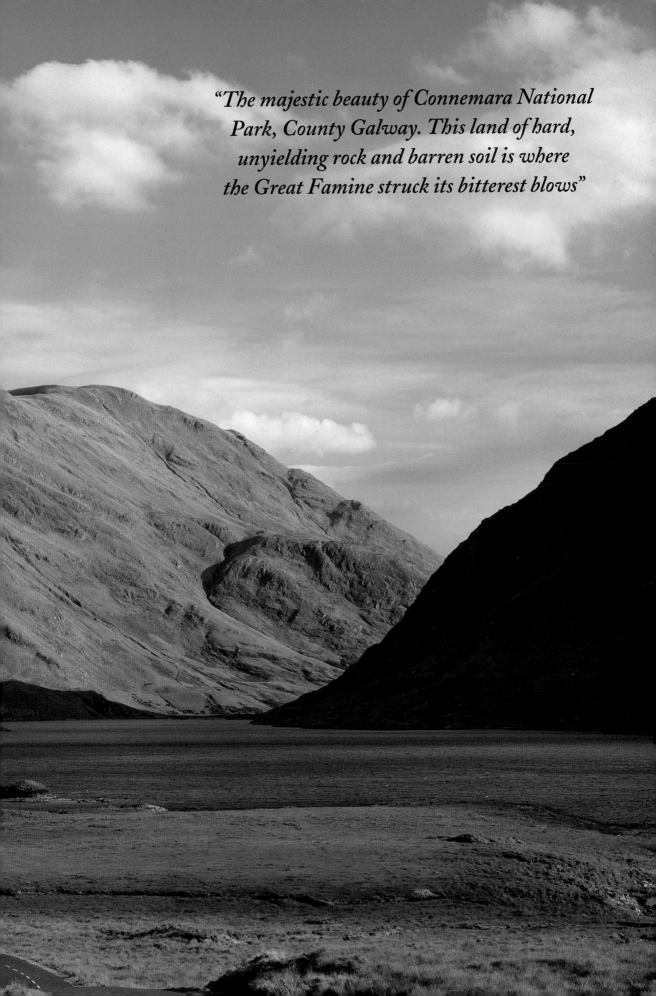

"*The majestic beauty of Connemara National Park, County Galway. This land of hard, unyielding rock and barren soil is where the Great Famine struck its bitterest blows*"

Galway to Sligo

So, once more, the open road beckons, and regretfully leaving Mayo and lovely Leitrim behind, we're on the way to Sligo, making for a beautiful stretch of beach for a moving, triumphant happening. It's called a 'Dip in the Nip'. I couldn't be there for the Big Dip itself, so I had the honour of starting it from the BBC Radio Theatre in London, where I was presenting my live music show, *Weekend Wogan*, before an audience I had placated, as usual, with sweets, biscuits and cake. A far cry from a windswept beach in Sligo, with a chill Atlantic sea. They rigged up a public address system among the sand dunes, and at the appointed hour I interrupted my show to say: 'We stop the roar of London's traffic, because on a beach far, far away in the county of Sligo, in the west of Ireland, a fine body of brave women stand, wrapped in

Mannin Bay, Connemara. Secluded sandy beaches, wild unspoilt countryside... reminds me of the Da's famous saying about eating the scenery!

their towels, ready and willing to brave the freezing elements and, dropping the towels, fling themselves into the bracing briny, on behalf of creating greater awareness and support of breast cancer. They call it a "Dip in the Nip" and it's my privilege to launch these wonderful women at the Atlantic breakers. So, ladies and gentlemen of the Radio Theatre audience, please join me in the countdown: three, two, one… Go!'

The ladies launched themselves; I claimed I could hear the splashes and cries of pain from London, but a month or so later, I saw for myself when the ladies did it again, just for me… and the five million viewers of *Terry Wogan's Ireland*, the better to publicise their deeply felt cause. I talked to the woman who started it all, Moira: 'I'm not sure that the Dip in the Nip could have happened even five years ago, in Ireland. I used to go to Donegal for holidays when I was a kid, and on the beach you kept yourself well wrapped up, not because of the cold but in the interests of Irish prudery. You walked right down to the water's edge wrapped up, cast off your towel and dived in. When you came out, you wrapped yourself up again, as quickly as your shivering body would allow. There was no real freedom in it, and when I organised the Dip for the first time, I had to remind the ladies that it was a fundraiser for breast cancer, because it became about something else – it became about a sense of liberation… Public nudity is still illegal in Ireland, and the Gardaí [Irish police] came along to help us make sure that everybody's privacy is protected, when they should be arresting us. An Irish solution to an Irish problem.'

I talked to some of the Dippers: 'It's my mother's ninetieth birthday, and she has breast cancer, so she didn't want presents – she wanted people to do something for the charity. This is my birthday present to her'.

'At first, we said we'd join in for a bit of craic, but our brother died of cancer last month, so we're doing the Dip for him. I'm sure that he's looking down on us now and laughing his head off.'

If you're not Irish and haven't been brought up there in the last century under the steely eyes of parish priests, Christian Brothers and Sisters of Charity, you'll have little idea of the iron rules of Catholic modesty under which we lived then. Our Catholicism was not the free and easy, liberal Church of the Mediterranean.

ABOVE: *On a Sligo beach, the brave ladies bare all for their cause*

LEFT: *Another beach, Sandymount, on Dublin Bay. Mark well the knitted swimsuit… very fashionable in its day*

Probably for historical reasons of fierce repression and persecution, the Irish Church became rigid, unyielding in its unquestioned rule. And lack of modesty was well up there with sex and vanity as a flagrant rejection of Irish Catholic values. I'm not sure if it didn't outrank murder…

Every summer, my great friend Bill Hayes's family invited me to join them in their seaside cottage, overlooking the lovely crescent beach of Kilkee, County Clare. Nobody undressed on that beach, either. You got into your swimming togs in the privacy of your house, wrapped yourself in your dressing gown or overcoat, and, towel in hand, walked virtually into the sea before discarding your wrapping. As Moira said, it tended to knock the fun out of it. Along from the beach were large pools in the rock, called the Pollock Holes. The three biggest were favourite spots for those who fancied a swim but without sand all over their toes. Naturally, the Pollock Holes had their rules, unspoken but ignored at your peril. The nearest, shrewdly named the first Pollock Hole, was for children. The second was for women. Just beyond it was a sign painted on a large rock: NO WOMEN BEYOND THIS POINT. For the largest Pollock Hole, the third, was for men only. Here, men could disport themselves in the nude safely away from the scandalised prying eyes of women. And although that was a long time ago, and Ireland and Irish society now much more liberated in their attitudes, I still found the Dip in the Nip a moving experience, a joyful expression of free spirit, finally loosening the stays of repression.

There were three main Pollock Holes, and it was a brave woman who strayed beyond the second one to the third, sacred to the naked male

Ben Bulben

In the words of the great poet, it was 'Horseman, pass by' in 'Yeats Country' as well. Our time in Sligo (the wife's mother's birthplace) was spent with those wonderful ladies making their brave and bold statement in the cold Atlantic, rather than 'Under bare Ben Bulben's head', the house at Lissadell, and the little churchyard where the great Willie Yeats lies at rest.

My friend, Kits Browning, son of Daphne du Maurier, took me to task over this grievous omission, and another old pal, the athlete, sportsman, writer and poet, and, if it comes to that, Ireland's last renaissance man, Ulick O'Connor, put it even more forcefully in an Irish newspaper: 'How could Terry, who knows hundreds of poems off by heart [so do a lot of Irish people, by the way. We were taught to recite poetry, not necessarily to appreciate it], have stood at the foot of Ben Bulben mountain and resisted reciting Yeats' famous lines, inscribed on his gravestone in the nearby Drumcliff graveyard?'

Oh, all right then, if it's not too late to repeat them here:

Under bare Ben Bulben's head
In Drumcliff churchyard Yeats is laid.
An ancestor was rector there...
Cast a cold eye
On life, on death.
Horseman, pass by!

Am I forgiven?

LEFT: *The tombstone of William Butler Yeats in the churchyard at Drumcliff, County Sligo, in the shadow of his beloved Ben Bulben*

"*Sheep take to the road in lovely Donegal, the most northerly county in the whole island of Ireland and a popular haunt for holidaying Dubliners*"

Sligo to Derry/ Londonderry

Reluctantly, we leave the beach and the ladies behind, and on past Sligo town, but always in sight of the massive bulk of Ben Bulben, beloved of Yeats. The north face is one of Ireland's most challenging climbs, and the mountain's flat top one of the country's most isolated and inhospitable places. A bizarre plateau, it's said that the remains of an American aircraft that crashed here during World War Two can still be found on its windswept surface.

Still heading north, we're in Donegal, a county in the Republic of Ireland that, in true Irish style, is more northerly than any in Northern Ireland. A favourite place for Dubliners to have their summer holiday cottages, it was somewhere I always hoped to avoid while working for the Royal Bank of Ireland Ltd. I had joined that bank specifically because it had fewer branches

Binevenagh Mountain, in the lowlands of northern County Derry/Londonderry. On a good day the views from the summit stretch as far as the Scottish coast

in country areas than others, and I wished to stay close to the comforts of home. However, the Royal Bank had branches in Donegal, in remote spots such as Moville and Dunfanaghy. Beautiful places, but, in the tradition of the Da, I felt that scenery was all very fine in its own way, but you can have too much of a good thing.

An abandoned police post on the border, all that remains of a once formidable array of security that bristled with checkpoints and watchtowers

So on we go, ever northwards, to cross the border between the two sovereign states that divide this little big island, from the Republic of Ireland to Britain, or, as it's known here, Northern Ireland. For ninety years, since Partition was agreed between Ireland and Britain, a border has existed between the twenty-six counties of Ireland and the six of the North. It has always been a bone of contention for Republicans and, until the Good Friday Agreement and power-sharing of a few years ago, a dangerous dividing line between two countries. When I last crossed this line, it bristled with gun emplacements, checkpoints, watchtowers, soldiers and police. I remember, in a Northern Ireland market town, watching British soldiers in full battle-gear making their way cautiously through shoppers, children, women with prams.

The Peace Agreement has brought that terrible dark time in our history to a merciful close, and now the soldiers patrol the busy streets no more; and on the border, the barbed wire, the checkpoints and the watchtowers are gone. You'd be hard-pressed to say where the border is any more, if it wasn't for the bureaux de change that turn the Irish euro into the British pound. The road signs are the other giveaway, suddenly changing from kilometres to miles. So, from one country that, at least until fairly recently, was an enthusiastic member state of the European Community, to one that is, perhaps, not quite so enthusiastic. And on the River Foyle, Northern Ireland's biggest city, the one with two names, depending on your political leaning – Derry/Londonderry. Or as my friend, the great Irish broadcaster Gerry Anderson, has put it so memorably – Stroke City.

So, what's the difference? Ask Gerry: 'You'd be stopped at night and somebody would say, "Where are you going?", and you'd answer, "Derry", wondering if you were right, because if you say "Derry" it means that you're probably a Catholic, but if you say "Londonderry" you're most definitely a Protestant. So, the fellow knows instantly what religion you are – important here during The Troubles.'

'The Troubles' – that's the Irish euphemism to end them all. It covers murder, terrorism, bombings, shootings, the loss of hundreds of innocent lives, kidnapping and extortion.

It was in Derry/Londonderry that I learned that in Northern Ireland it's not what side of the tracks you were born, but which side of the river. It's over a decade since the Peace Agreement was signed, but the River Foyle which runs through the town still acts

The historic walls of Derry, defended by the Protestant apprentice boys against a Catholic force

as a kind of no-man's-land, separating the Catholics on the west bank of the river from the Protestants on the east bank, with just one bridge connecting the two communities.

The historic walls of the old city were originally built by English and Scottish Protestant settlers to make the native Catholics keep their distance, and are famed in song and story; and, as ever in this part of the country, commemorated with marches and drums, as the place where Protestant apprentice boys bravely defended the walls against a Catholic force, and won the day. As we walked the walls of Derry, Gerry Anderson, long a fearless commentator on Northern Ireland's 'Troubles', and in particular those of what he calls 'Stroke City', explained how the time-bomb of four centuries of religious discrimination was finally ignited, in 1947: 'The big mistake by those in power was allowing Catholics to receive secondary education for the first time. This was the very

A common sight in Northern Ireland, murals have for decades been used to document the province's troubled times. These murals in Free Derry are in remembrance of Bloody Sunday

The great man of 'Stroke City', Gerry Anderson, and I walk Derry's walls in the rain...

first generation of Catholics to be made aware of just how unfairly they'd been treated over the centuries. The guys who would not normally get an education said, "Hold on a minute. I've been treated here like a second-class citizen..." So, by the time people who are twelve years old in 1947 get to university, it's 1959, perhaps '60. They leave university at twenty-one, look around them, live a little, and then they're twenty-five or twenty-six by the time they realise that something has to be done. Oh, look – it's 1969! Time to start "The Troubles"...'

I left Ireland for Britain in late 1969, and broadcast daily on BBC Radio 2 throughout Northern Ireland's worst years of terror and killings. When the IRA brought their bombing campaign to Britain, it made life very difficult for the millions of Irish people, of several generations, who had made their lives happily there, having integrated successfully over many years into British society. I always think that it was because of that integration that the British didn't react more violently to the Irish in their midst. Almost every British person had a friend or neighbour or even a relative who was Irish, whom they had known and liked for years. I'm sure it softened what might have been a source of discrimination, and even violence. Certainly, I felt it a tribute to British tolerance that I continued to broadcast every morning to the nation, while violence and killing was being done in my country's name, although not, as I made clear, in mine. To speak cheerfully to millions of British people the morning after some of my countrymen had killed several of their innocent countrymen with a bomb in a pub was something I will never forget.

It has been a source of pride for me that Irish people who lived in Britain during the bad times have thanked me for the comfort I brought to them then, and the reassurance that it was all right to be Irish, and proud of it. I was privileged and, therefore, personally suffered no violence, or even insult, but a large parcel was sent to me at the BBC. The way it was then, the parcel was inspected by the post-room security and, when X-rayed, found to contain explosives. The Special Branch were informed and Broadcasting House immediately cordoned off. As, indeed, were Upper Regent Street and Oxford Circus. The inconvenience to everybody in the BBC, not to mention the thousands of London commuters, shoppers, bus passengers and motorists, for a couple of hours until the bomb was defused, was enormous. I didn't feel a thing; completely unaffected by the chaos – I was on holiday. Whoever sent the device couldn't have been much of a fan…

Gerry Anderson, who has always spoken freely and fairly to both sides of the Derry divide, has had more threats and insults than an English football manager, but he remains irrepressibly cheerful, witty, and an ever-honest observer. As we continued our walk along the mighty walls, we looked down on the little houses, and there, the murals that tell of the troubled times, with their slogans and graphics. And they tell of that terrible day, 30 January 1972 – Bloody Sunday. There's another Bloody Sunday in Ireland's history, when, some fifty years before, in retaliation for the assassination of British agents by Michael Collins' IRA, the British army broke through the gates of Croke Park, Dublin, where an All-Ireland final was being held, and turned their guns on the innocent crowd, killing many. And, in a dreadful parallel, so it was that Sunday in Derry. A civil rights march through the city ended in tragedy when thirteen demonstrators were shot dead by British soldiers. A fourteenth died later. All were Catholics.

It took thirty-eight years, but after an investigation led by Lord Saville the truth was finally unravelled in 2010, with the conclusion that the deaths were 'unjustified and unjustifiable'. After years of excuses and whitewashing, the Supreme Court finally concluded that the fourteen Catholics had not been posing any threat to the peace, or the army. I'll let Gerry Anderson tell it: 'The Saville Report was the first time that anything happened that was really positive, because somebody was coming out with the statement, "You were right, those people were innocent." It gave the city a tremendous boost of self-confidence. And our only response was, "Thank you, that's all we want."'

The Saville report sent a wave of hope and optimism through the city, boosting the existing initiatives to help bring together the next generation of Catholics and Protestants in this town. In the past, the Creggan housing estate on the outskirts of the town has been a breeding ground for unrest and terrorism, but now it stages one of Europe's biggest youth football tournaments, the Foyle Cup. It attracts top under-eighteen footballers from throughout these islands and Europe, and has become a favourite hunting ground for new talent for spotters from the big clubs. We watched a game between Derry City and St Kevins, from Dublin, and afterwards I spoke to a local player, Loughlain Toland, who told me that things were much more peaceful around the Creggan now than when he was growing up. He thought a lot of that was down to the football, to Catholic and Protestant boys playing against each other. It's a step forward, and hopefully a positive one away from the

Jubilation at the result of the Saville Report, thirty-eight years after the events of Bloody Sunday

An artist's impression of the Peace Bridge. The two banks of the Foyle united at last

discrimination, the medieval religious prejudices and hatreds that have poisoned the Foyle for far too long. They are even building a new bridge across the river, to link the two banks so long separated by more than water. It's the biggest regeneration project in the city for over thirty years. It will be called the Peace Bridge.

As I write this, it's well over a year since I bade my loyal listeners to my daily morning radio show a reluctant farewell, but as I said at the time, I've always preferred to make my own way to the exit rather than be led there. These were my parting words:

> This is it then – the day I've been dreading, the inevitable morning when you and I come to the parting of the ways, the last *Wake Up to Wogan*. It wasn't always thus; for the first twelve years it was the plain old *Terry Wogan Show*, and you were all TWITS, the Terry Wogan Is Tops Society. When I returned to the bosom of our family, it became *Wake Up to Wogan*, and you all became TOGS, Terry's Old Geezers and Gals. It's always been a source of enormous pride to me that you've come together in my name, that you're proud to call yourselves my listeners, that you think of me as a friend, someone that you're close enough to laugh with, to poke fun at, and occasionally, when the world seemed just a little cruel, to shed a tear

with. The years together with you have not only been a pleasure, but a privilege. You've allowed me to share your lives with you, and when you tell me how important I've been in your lives, it's very moving, and humbling. You've been every bit as important to mine… We've been through at least a couple of generations together, for many of you, your children, like mine, now have children of their own… Your support for Children in Need has been consistent and magnificent. You've baked the cakes, held the quizzes, sold the calendars, packed the CDs and DVDs, answered the phones, always there when I've called on you, unheralded, unsung. If anyone embodies the generous, warm spirit of this country, it's you, my listener. I'm not going to pretend this is not a sad day. I'm going to miss the laughter, the fun of our mornings together. I know that you're going to welcome Chris Evans with the same generosity of spirit that you've always shown me. I'm going to miss you, till we're together again, in February. Thank you for being my friend.

'I thought he'd never go…'

"*The Sperrins – the largest and least explored mountain range in Northern Ireland, stretching along the border between Tyrone and Derry/Londonderry. Desolate yet, at the same time, beautiful*"

Derry/Londonderry to Enniskillen

Father Brian D'Arcy was a regular contributor to *Wake Up to Wogan* from its very beginning, but he's been a good friend of mine since before I left Ireland. He conducted the funeral services of both my mother and father, and, along with his fellow contributor to 'Pause for Thought' on BBC Radio 2, Canon Roger Royle ('The Loose Canon'), celebrated the services and Mass of the marriages of my three children. Father Brian is a very modern Irish priest, whose opinions as a journalist and on television and radio have not always endeared him to the Irish Catholic hierarchy.

I met him first when he was the parish priest of Mount Argus church in Dublin. From there he moved to a parish in Northern Ireland, then to work in the townships of South Africa, before taking charge of The Graan, a monastery in Enniskillen, County

Monea Castle, County Fermanagh. Now a State Care Historic Monument, it was once the home of the governor of Enniskillen

Fermanagh, also known as St Gabriel's Retreat. With the help of his marvellous lady parishioners, he has made a real haven of The Graan, not only for those who attend Mass, or come for advice and solace, but his elderly fellow Passionist priests. Brian used to broadcast live, on what's called an ISDN line, from his bedroom and, looking out his window, keep me abreast on the 'duck's foot' weather raining down on Enniskillen and the health of the cattle in an adjoining field. So, according to him, he'd pop out of bed at ten past eight, link up with BBC London, deliver himself of some uplifting thoughts, wish us all a good day and God bless, and straight back into bed... A likely story.

I've never met a priest who works harder on his mission of pastoral care than Father Brian D'Arcy. He ranges Ireland from north to south in his ministry, pausing only to watch his favourite game, Gaelic football, and listen, as he goes, to his favourite music, country and western. Because of his love of popular music, in the sixties and seventies Brian became friend, and often moral and spiritual adviser, to many of Ireland's musical phenomenon of the time, the showbands. For two decades, the showbands dominated the Irish pop scene, bringing their brand of live music to every 'Ballroom of Romance', from Cork to Belfast, from Dublin to Galway. Ballrooms sprang up everywhere, and the middle of nowhere, to cater for the demand for music and dance in the Irish

Showbands were all the rage in Ireland in the sixties and seventies. The Pacific Showband... and nun!

A fresh-faced young jock at the microphone of Radios 1 and 2. Don't ask me about the shirt...

countryside. Young men and women cycled for miles to dance to the Royal Showband, the Clipper Carltons, the Dixielanders, the Freshmen, the Miami and a thousand others. You'd pass what looked like a large airport hangar in the middle of a field, surrounded by hundreds upon hundreds of bicycles, the odd car, and the coach that was going to carry the band the following night to their next gig, probably at the other end of the country.

I had hardly started to work for BBC Radios 1 and 2 before a great scandal shook the Old Lady to her very stays. Some presenters and producers were found to have taken bribes, both monetary and sexual, to play certain artistes' records on their shows. I still don't know whether to be flattered or insulted that nobody offered me anything. It would have been nice to have been at least tested. It was known as 'payola', and I have to confess to having experienced the Irish showband version while working for Radio Éireann. I used to present *Hospitals Requests*, a much-listened-to music show that helped to popularise the showbands' records. One day, just before I went on the air, a showband manager came into the office. He presented me with a copy of his band's latest record and then, with the skill of a sleight-of-hand artist, produced a packet of cigarettes and laid it on my table. 'Now,' he said slyly, 'they're for yourself.' I don't smoke, so even that was hardly a test of my moral fibre.

Outside the calm of his peaceful monastery, Father Brian works his wonders in a troubled world. In 2009, the Murphy Report, after years of whitewash, cover-up and blatant lying

denial, confirmed that there had been a number of cases of child abuse by Catholic priests in Dublin from at least the 1970s. This most devoutly Catholic of countries has had its trust and confidence in the Church seriously undermined. Brian D'Arcy has been a very public critic of the way his Church has handled these revelations, but to talk about it he brought me to his favourite place, beautiful Lough Erne. It helps that he's been a lifelong pal of the boatman, Pat Lunny, who takes us out on the huge, tranquil lake. This is the place that Brian claims has kept him 'reasonably sane'. I asked him if he came here to reflect, or just to look at the lapping waves of Lough Erne and think of nothing.

'I think both are the same thing,' he said. 'This lake has always been a holy place, long before Christianity. Then, at the very beginning of the Christian faith, Saints Melash and Devenish, the great Columbanus of Iona, all came here to reflect and pray. It was one of the places that made Ireland almost the last bastion of faith and learning during the Dark Ages that followed the fall of the Roman Empire, and led to the country being called "The Island of Saints and Scholars". It gives me a feeling of spirituality that seems to be missing elsewhere in the new Ireland.'

ABOVE LEFT: *A dear friend, and a man who epitomises the true spirit of Christianity, Father Brian D'Arcy shares his thoughts as we cross the waters of his beloved Lough Erne*

ABOVE: *A scene of utter serenity: dawn on Upper Lough Erne*

*While I had to get up at all
hours to make my way
to the BBC studios for my
Radio 2 morning show,
Father Brian tumbled out
of his bed to the microphone*

"Slemish Mountain, in County Antrim, dominates the landscape for miles around. According to legend, Slemish is the first known Irish home of St Patrick. It was during his time here that he is said to have found God"

BELFAST

Enniskillen

DUBLIN

Enniskillen to Belfast

When I was a young man, people from the south very rarely crossed the border into Northern Ireland. More people came in the other direction, but they were mostly Catholic/Nationalist, holidaying in the Republic to get away from the Protestant/ Unionist triumphalism of the 'marching season', the drums and fifes of the Orange Order, celebrating the victory of King Billy at the Battle of the Boyne, four hundred years ago. There was a rail link between Dublin and Belfast, but it's evidence of the former disconnection between the two cities that they've only just completed the final section of a new motorway between them. As a boy, I only went to Belfast to play rugby against school teams there, although my mother, Rose, was born there, in a British army barracks. For her father, Frank Byrne, was a sergeant major

The Crom Estate, County Fermanagh, is an important nature reserve, not far from Enniskillen. There are ruins and ancient yew trees, and you might even be fortunate enough to see a rare pine marten

Belfast's famous cranes, Samson and Goliath, at Harland and Wolff docks

in the Dublin Fusiliers. When he moved back to Beggars Bush barracks in Dublin, the family moved with him. Sadly, he died before I was able to ask him about his service to king and country, whether he'd fought in the Boer War, or been involved in the Irish Uprising of 1916. But I do have a photograph of the bold Frank Byrne in uniform, and I detect a certain family resemblance.

The Belfast I knew as a young man was, even then, the home of the world's biggest shipbuilders, Harland and Wolff. Two monstrous yellow cranes, symbols of global supremacy, still bestride the shipyards. They're known as Samson and Goliath, and for many Catholics in Northern Ireland they stand as symbols of another kind of supremacy, for although Harland and Wolff once employed over thirty thousand people, very few were Catholics.

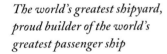

The world's greatest shipyard, proud builder of the world's greatest passenger ship

As the world's biggest shipbuilders, it was only fitting that the Belfast shipyard would build the world's largest passenger ship. There's a huge, empty space in this dockyard, where the *Titanic* was built. On 10 April 1912, to the cheers of the workers and the waving of flags, the great ship set sail for New York. She stopped in Cobh, and a couple of days later struck an iceberg in mid-Atlantic. The tragedy has been documented often enough, but what is less well known is that of the fifteen hundred people who drowned, twenty-two were local Ulstermen. Their lives are commemorated by the Titanic Memorial in the grounds of Belfast City Hall. Thomas Millar's story is typical of the ordinary Irishmen who had the misfortune to be aboard the great ship when it sank. Susie Millar is his great-granddaughter. She showed me a picture of Thomas, taken when he was thirty-three, his ambitions and future all ahead of him. She told me his story:

'Thomas Millar worked as an engine fitter, and for the three years it took to complete *Titanic*, he watched the ship get bigger and bigger, thinking about the sort of places it would be going and all the opportunities it would offer. So he set about improving himself, and studied to become a sea-going engineer, or marine engineer. But just three months before *Titanic* sailed, his wife died. Thomas was left with two young children. He wanted to give them the best start in life, so he signed up with White Star, and off he went on the *Titanic* with the idea of getting to America, and when he got work, sending for his two boys.'

Susie told me that, as a deck engineer, Thomas would have

been responsible for the mechanisms that controlled the lifeboats, so in all probability his job as the ship went down was to get people into the boats and lower them into the sea. There would, of course, have been no place for him or the crew in the lifeboats, so the poor man went down with the ship. Seeking to do good for himself and his children, instead he left them orphaned. As we stood over the empty dock, Susie told me the final twist in the sad tale: 'This very place where we're standing would have been the last place that my grandfather saw his father. Before he sailed, Thomas took my grandfather aside and gave him two pennies, saying, "Don't spend these until I see you again." My grandfather kept the two pennies all his life.'

Susie showed them to me. The head of George V, 1912. The sinking of the *Titanic* was the darkest day in the history of the Belfast shipyards, but the ill-fated ship has given its name to a huge project to regenerate the entire docklands area: the Titanic Quarter. Just as with London's Docklands, it's going to include a new financial and business district, and a museum devoted to the memory of one of the twentieth century's greatest tragedies.

I visited the wonderful old building that once was the majestic world headquarters of Harland and Wolff. It's destined to become a *Titanic*-themed grand hotel. I just wanted to get a look before the developers move in. What a place this must have been, in Belfast's great shipbuilding days – majestic sweeping stairways, even aristocratic sanitary ware, reflective of a transatlantic liner.

Susie Millar tells me the sad story of her great-grandfather, Thomas (above), and the two pennies he left to her grandfather

The huge drawing office of Harland and Wolff, once the world's biggest shipbuilder

But the *pièces de résistance* are the huge, high-ceilinged, massive-windowed drawing offices, though dusty with age and lack of use still full of the light shed to help the draughtsmen, architects and artists who designed and drew the plans for many of the twentieth century's greatest liners and ships.

I talked to two old H and W hands, John Higgins and Rodney McCullough, about how it was in the still-palmy days of the fifties and sixties, when they both worked here. At that time, the great shipbuilder was employing more than fifty thousand people all over Britain, with Belfast still the major workforce of thirty thousand-plus and the hub of the H and W empire. According to John, everything in the offices was very disciplined. You didn't clock in, you had a little block of wood with a number stamped across the top. You collected that number in the morning from the time-keeper and handed it back at night as you left. The board was crucial, used even when you went to the toilet. There was a time-keeper there, too, who took your board as you entered and in seven minutes would come and rattle the toilet door to tell you that your time was up. The toilets at Harland and Wolff were therefore known as 'minutes', because that's all you got to do what you had to do… Still, seven minutes, that should be time enough.

Unfortunately, time ran out for the Belfast shipyard. But it seems to be rising again, phoenix-like, from the ashes. Let's hope that the 'Titanic Experience' will restore it to a different glory.

ABOVE LEFT: *Another view of the great drawing office, with its vast windows that let in light to assist the draughtsmen in their work*

Belfast is overlooked by two towering mountains, Divis and Black, which form a dramatic backdrop to the city

"The Ring of Gullion, Area of Outstanding Natural Beauty. The rich, fertile land and rolling hills of County Armagh belie its recent violent history"

Belfast to
South Armagh

Fifty miles south of Belfast, Armagh is one of Northern Ireland's four border counties. Rich, fertile land, rolling hills, a gentle landscape that belies its recent violent history. South Armagh is closest to the border. In fact, on its little winding roads you could find yourself in and out of Northern Ireland several times in a couple of miles. And not for nothing was it known as 'bandit country'. During the three decades of The Troubles, some two hundred and fifty people were killed in South Armagh.

We've come to the township of Jonesborough, once regarded by British forces and the police as an IRA stronghold, with those twisting roads and wooded hillsides impossible to fully secure. Nowadays, thankfully, it's a much different story. The only indicator of what might be described as explosive violence is the shop

Orchard County: blossom on the apple trees in County Armagh

LEFT: *'There's no line in a map, with music'*

BOTTOM LEFT: *St Brigid's Accordion Band in all their glory, proud All-Ireland champions*

BELOW: *The spirit of Ireland's reconciliation between North and South*

that sells fireworks. On the Northern Ireland side of the border, of course – fireworks are illegal in the Republic. Although if you're from the southern side, all you've got to do is cross the road.

Jonesborough has about two hundred people living in the area, eighty of whom play the accordion. I doubt if you'd find such a statistic anywhere else in the world, including France or Italy. I've always thought accordion-playing a dying art, reserved for the more arcane performances of the Eurovision Song Contest, but the instrument is not only alive and well here, it's positively rampant. The St Brigid's Accordion Band has members not only from both sides of the border, but from both sides of the religious divide. Siobhan, the moving spirit behind this accordion madness, started it from nothing in 1991 with her brother and sister and a lady from across the border. She couldn't tell me why they decided to make it an accordion, rather than a banjo, tin whistle or fife and drum band. For Siobhan, the old squeeze-box was

king, easy to listen to, versatile and affordable. But not that easy to play. So Siobhan, and those that could, gave lessons and soon they were up to the epaulettes of their pretty marching costumes in young volunteers.

You have to understand that, for young people, there's not a lot else going on in Jonesborough. But you can become part of a band that has won the All-Ireland Championship three times in a row, and five times altogether, and has competed with the best at international level. Breege, Siobhan's daughter, is a university graduate but has come back to play in the band. She takes a young educated person's view, one that will hopefully grow: 'Culturally, the only difference between the North and the South is that the postboxes are green down there and red up here. And there's no line in a map, with music.'

The St Brigid's Accordion Band marches proudly down Jonesborough's only street, drums beating, even a portable xylophone chiming, but rising above it all, the melodious music of forty accordions playing as one. One of Northern Ireland's most hopeful sounds.

ABOVE LEFT: *Our hero striding manfully over Ireland's four green fields*

*Carlingford Lough, on the
border between Northern
Ireland and the Republic.
People may not come to
Ireland for the weather,
but when the sun shines...*

"Knowth passage-grave, the largest in the Brú na Bóinne complex. In the Boyne Valley area there are three major Neolithic sites – Knowth, Newgrange and Tara"

BELFAST

Armagh

DUBLIN

South Armagh to Dublin

A step across the street and we're in the Republic, heading towards some of all Ireland's most historic sites. I know that there's a popular saying that the Irish think they're the only people that history ever happened to, but around the Boyne Valley they've got reason. In this area are three major Neolithic sites, Newgrange, Knowth and Tara – the last named, also the site of the fort from which the High King of Ireland ruled. As you stand on the old earthworks, you can see why – look north, and in the misty distance, the Mountains of Mourne, deep in Ulster; look south, and there's Dublin Bay. Not much went on, on Ireland's east coast, that wasn't under the eagle eye of the High King. At Newgrange is sited the most spectacular example of a Neolithic passage-grave in Europe, dating from around 3200BC. It's been beautifully preserved, and

The Boyne – where the Protestant force of William of Orange defeated the Catholic army of James Stuart. That was in 1690 but for some diehards it might have been yesterday

Pre-dating the Pyramids, the Neolithic passage-grave of Newgrange

to this day you can crawl down the long stone passage, decorated with spirals and zigzags, to the burial chamber. Newgrange was designed by its builders so that the sun could enter the chamber only once a year, on midwinter day, which suggests that these ancient people may have had a knowledge of astronomy, and may even have been sun-worshippers.

But what these people believed, indeed who they were, where they came from, where they learned their building skills, remain mysteries of Ireland's prehistoric past. The Gaels, a Celtic people, had taken over the country by the first century BC, but according to the Greek geographer, Strabo, were 'more savage than the Britons, feed on human flesh and are enormous eaters'. He probably never got near the country, because what evidence we have shows that the Celts, the Gaels, were a highly sophisticated society, and four centuries later the High King, Cormac mac Airt, built schools at Tara for the study of law, literature and military science. He also didn't neglect himself or his social duties, building an enormous palace which was described in the *Book of Leinster*, nine hundred years later, as having a banqueting hall seven hundred feet long.

There's a statue to Ireland's patron saint, Patrick, in a prominent position on the Hill of Tara, but he was a good two hundred years after Cormac mac Airt, and under Patrick's Christian influence Tara became a religious centre. It has always held a mystic

The Hill of Tara, from where Ireland's High Kings ruled

grip on the Irish imagination: in 1798, thousands of Irish rebels spontaneously assembled there, and in 1843 almost a million gathered at Tara to hear 'The Liberator', Daniel O'Connell, whose political skills and oratory had won Catholic Emancipation for the Irish. Tara has always epitomised Ireland's lost Gaelic glory. As the nineteenth-century poet, Thomas Moore, put it:

> *The harp that once through Tara's halls*
> *The soul of music shed,*
> *Now hangs as mute on Tara's walls,*
> *As if that soul were fled.*

To the Celts, with their druidic beliefs, the Boyne was a divine river, and so, to this day, it remains to some Orangemen and Unionists in Northern Ireland. On every twelfth of July, they march to pipes and huge drums to celebrate the Battle of the Boyne in 1690, and the great triumph of the Protestant army led by William of Orange over the Catholic forces of James II. If we want to be picky, it was fought on the first of July, which became the twelfth when the calendar was changed in the eighteenth century. Also, when Pope Innocent XI heard of the victory, he ordered a Te Deum to be sung in the Vatican in praise of the Williamites. Apparently, James Stuart and his ally, Louis XIV of France, were a greater menace to the Catholic Church at the time than William of Orange.

The Battle of the Boyne remains the only significant battle in European terms ever fought in Ireland. Thirty thousand Catholic troops marched up from the south, and forty thousand down from the north. Apart from the numerical superiority, King Billy's men were hardened veterans of European wars. James's followers were mainly farmers and, according to the historian, the splendidly named Turtle Bunbury, whom I spoke to, the brandy rations of the Jacobites were a contributory factor. These arrived on the morning of the battle itself, and unsurprisingly proved to have a debilitating effect. Some histories have it that the battle was not particularly hard-fought, with James distinguishing himself by retreating first. There's a story of a Lady Tyrconnell, on hearing King James condemn his Irish soldiers for running away, pointedly remarking: 'But Your Majesty won the race.'

It was a poor example of a 'not particularly hard-fought battle' if what I heard in Malahide Castle, just outside Dublin, is true. On the morning of the Battle of the Boyne, twelve men sat down to breakfast in the great hall there. None ever returned. There's a huge painting of the battle in that same dining room and, on the wall leading to the staircase, a portrait of one of my ancestors, who used to own the historic pile. They say that there's a striking family resemblance to yours truly, but that's little consolation. Who took my castle, and reduced poor old great-grandfather Michael Wogan to mending Lord Powerscourt's boots?

After King Billy's great victory, the Jacobites and their Irish

Catholic followers retreated to Limerick and made their final stand there. Limerick has been known ever since as the City of the Broken Treaty, and with good reason. The treaty guaranteed the rights and property of the defeated Irish, in return for loyalty to William and Mary. About eleven thousand Catholic officers and men were allowed to sail into exile to join the Irish Brigade of the French army. There was probably a Wogan or two among them for, later on, a certain Chevalier Charles Wogan cut a bit of a swathe, rescuing Princess Marie Sobieski from imprisonment and carrying her to Edinburgh to marry. She became the mother of Bonnie Prince Charlie, and your man Wogan, eventually, the governor of La Mancha province in Spain. Or maybe that was another Wogan… Certainly there was a Baron de Wogan in France; I have pictorial evidence of my brave ancestor, decked out in furs on a bleak Canadian shore. And another bleaker prospect, tied to a totem pole, while the Iroquois, or possibly Huron, decide whether or not to scalp his large moustache.

Anyway, the treaty was broken before the ink was dry by the

The Baron de Wogan, whose outrageous moustaches seem to have inflamed the native Americans

Irish Parliament, now entirely Protestant, and Viscount Sydney, the Lord Lieutenant, smartly dispossessed four thousand Catholic landowners. In 1695 the legislation known as the 'Penal Laws' came into force. No Catholic could own a gun or a sword; Catholic bishops were banned and banished; no Catholic could buy land nor inherit it from a Protestant. The estates of a Catholic landowner were to be divided equally among his sons, unless one of them converted to Protestantism, in which case he inherited the lot. Catholics were banned from entering a profession, or receiving a formal education. A Catholic could not own a horse worth more than a pound. From a modern perspective these laws are simply so disgraceful as to be ridiculous – but they lasted well over a hundred years.

*From O'Connell Street,
Limerick, to O'Connell Street,
Dublin – the Ma and me*

And so, once more, we turn the car's bonnet towards Dublin, just as the little Wogan family did, all those years ago, when the Da was rewarded for his intelligence and hard work by being offered the general managership of the Leverett & Frye grocery chain. An enormous step up for him; the realisation of a dream for the Ma, now just up the road from her beloved Muds and her sisters; just a change of scenery for the Brother, Brian, who was only eight years of age; but a complete sea change for a fifteen-year-old who was leaving all his friends behind, moving to a neighbourhood where he knew nobody and a school where everybody was a stranger. Actually, I don't remember it being all that traumatic; I knew Dublin pretty well after all those summer holidays with the Granny and the Aunties. I knew where all the cinemas were, and Cafolla's Ice Cream Parlour. I was closer, on a permanent basis, to a knickerbocker glory than I had been in the past; we had a telephone, and a car!

The Da had been taught to drive before he left Limerick by our good friend, and my hero, Gordon Wood. I'm proud to call Gordon's son, Keith, also an Irish international rugby player, my friend. A couple of years ago, we even ran a golf tournament together for charity, in Doonbeg, a truly magnificent course that complements another, Lahinch, a little further up the coast of County Clare. When I was last in Doonbeg, they were building houses along by the second fairway, and I went to have a look. All the workers' signs were in Polish. Hard to believe that immigrant

European workers would have found their way to the continent's remotest shore. Where are they now? Like the thousands of workers who came to Ireland during the boom years, probably back home.

The other unusual aspect of Doonbeg is a snail. A snail so small that it can scarcely be seen with the naked eye. But a rare snail, so rare that environmentalists insist that it be protected. So, a considerable acreage of the course is fenced off and out of bounds, and it is here that the little molluscs live and thrive. Or so they say, but it's hard to tell how well anything is doing if you can't see it. Suffice it to say that I feel guilty whenever I slice a drive into the little fellows' reserve. I must have killed hundreds...

Doonbeg. The Clare coast is full of great golf courses – this magnificent one is the latest, designed by Greg Norman. They say that if the ball bounces in the rough, you might well find it...

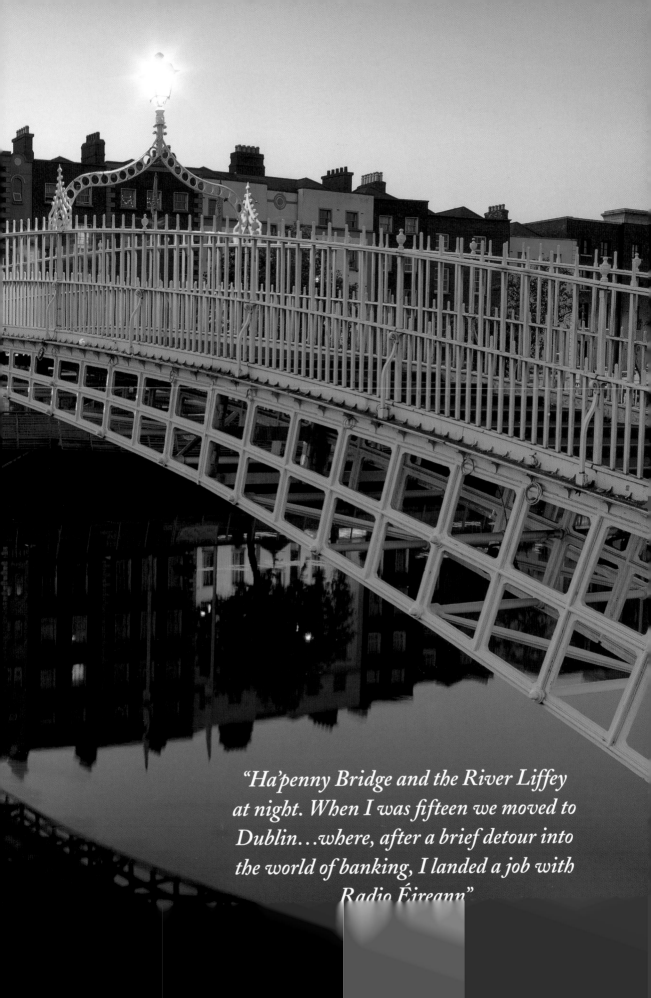

"Ha'penny Bridge and the River Liffey
at night. When I was fifteen we moved to
Dublin…where, after a brief detour into
the world of banking, I landed a job with
Radio Éireann"

BELFAST

DUBLIN

Dublin

So, the Wogans came to Dublin, and I stopped being a 'bogman' and became a 'Jackeen'. Dublin has traditionally been regarded by the Irish outside the Pale as an outpost of the British Empire, and Dublin people, therefore, little followers of the Union Jack – 'Jackeens'.

I didn't find the transition all that difficult: same type of school, same subjects, slightly better class of bicycle – well, it was a longer journey from Ballymun Avenue to Belvedere College, Dublin, than it was from 18, Elm Park to Crescent College, Limerick. I certainly found a difference at the weekends, no longer back and forward to Billy or James's house, no more games of Subbuteo. The closeness and friendship of a smaller place were gone. None of the friends that I found easy to make in the

Looking north from the bridge, the broad boulevard of O'Connell Street, Dublin

classrooms and rugby teams of Belvedere lived anywhere near me. In the two and a half years I spent there, I only remember being invited to visit a friend's home once. And he lived in Malahide, so I had to take a train, and stay overnight. No hardship; his mother cooked mushrooms for tea, a foreign and delicious taste for me – the fungus was unknown to my own dear Ma. She and my friend Ken's mother became firm friends, and would meet every so often, in their hats and coats, for tea at Bewley's in Dublin. They never made a foursome for dinner with their husbands, but then, going out to dinner was virtually unknown to our class of people, in the Ireland of the late fifties. Anyway, it was a mothers' meeting. And they never called each other by their first names – Birdie and Rose; it was Mrs Daly and Mrs Wogan throughout their years of friendship.

I was lucky, I suppose, to slot in so easily at a new school, although there was a moment of real fear, when I found that the terrifying prefect of studies, Father 'Snitch' McLoughlin, who ran Crescent College, Limerick, with an ascetic, iron hand, had followed me up to Dublin, to create fear and loathing at Belvedere. I warned my new classmates of the reign of terror that was to come, but in Dublin, in a bigger school, he never became quite the Torquemada he was in Limerick. The fact that I'd played rugby in Munster got me a place in the Belvedere senior team, which guaranteed a degree of status; that, and a couple of leading roles in the school's annual Gilbert and Sullivan extravaganzas, meant that I was generally accepted as not being a complete eejit. They were happy days at Belvedere – too happy – I didn't do half as well in my final exams there as I had in the intermediate tests at Crescent, where I had been driven to study largely by fear.

Another difference between living in Dublin rather than Limerick was that it was more difficult to tell Protestants from Catholics. Anyone who thinks that such discrimination only existed in Northern Ireland is sadly mistaken. In Limerick, we could tell a Protestant just by looking at them. It was called the 'Protestant Look'. You didn't have to know their names, or where they went to school (dead giveaways), and which side of the river you live is peculiar to Northern Ireland. No, in Limerick you could tell by their complexions: Anglo-Saxon, fair-skinned. I told

Dublin is full of statues to its great men and women – this is James Joyce, and Molly Malone with her basket of 'Cockles and mussels, alive, alive, oh!'

my wife Helen about this preposterous nonsense and she said, 'Yes, I thought that you were a Protestant when I met you first. You had The Look. And a funny name…'

It was around about this time that it struck someone in authority that there might be some mileage in earning a few bob for the country by encouraging people other than returning emigrants to visit Ireland. The first fruits of this brainwave were not all that encouraging; they called it 'An Tóstal', the Festival. For reasons lost in the mists of time, it opened in April, the wettest month of the year. It attracted few tourists, and a certain amount of resentment from the natives – particularly of an extraordinary artefact, boldly placed in the middle of O'Connell Street, Dublin, that was designed to sum up the spirit of An Tóstal. So it did, a huge bowl of plastic flames that shimmered day and night. Dubliners, not known for their excessive respect for the statuary that graces their fair city (Molly Malone's is known as 'The Tart with the Cart', James Joyce's as 'The P***k with the Stick'), thought the 'Bowl of Light' a monument to bad taste, and one night – and it must have taken a large number of discerning citizens – they threw it over the bridge, into the Liffey.

If anything characterised Dublin in the fifties, apart from the shouting and abuse of the fishwives in Moore Street Market ('This

Festivals

Festivals abound in Ireland. Music and folk festivals. Galway is given over all year to any reason they can think of for a bit of craic. Apart from the Macnas street festival and the annual beheading of King Charles, they have their Race Festival and, perhaps their biggest, the Galway Oyster Festival, the town awash with stout and platefuls of the old bi-valved mollusc.

There used to be the Kilkenny Beer Festival, which I hope is still bubbling, and the Wexford Opera Festival, which attracts the very cream of world operatic talent; and then there's Puck Fair, in Killorglin, County Kerry, which culminates in the puck – a large billy goat – being festooned in flowers and placed on a high platform for all to applaud. The goat so revered, it is thought, as a pagan symbol of fertility. I hope that the Dublin Theatre Festival continues to flourish, and all the drama festivals that were part of life in almost every small Irish town.

The Puck Fair, Killorglin, in the 1950s and more recently. They still pay homage there to 'the puck' – a billy goat

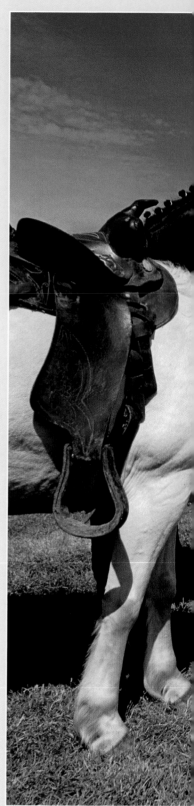

fish is very small.' 'What do you want for a shillin', Moby Dick?'),
it was the cinema queue. Every cinema, on and off O'Connell
Street – Savoy, Capitol, Adelphi, Metropole, Royal and all the
others – always had a long line outside it. Nobody at that time
in Dublin ever walked straight into a movie. You waited, without complaint, in all weathers, and then, when you got inside,
lined up along the aisle until a seat was vacated and it was your
turn. For years, I never saw a film from beginning to end, usually
coming and going somewhere in the middle. To this day, I never
have any trouble picking up the storylines of any television soap
opera, no matter at which point I join the drama.

One of the reasons for this compulsive queueing was that,
apart from the pub, there wasn't much else in the way of entertainment. Television didn't rear its head as a national service in
Ireland until the early sixties, although gradually, in the late fifties,
people began buying television sets and erecting huge aerials on
their roofs to pick up fringe reception, from Wales and Northern
Ireland, of British television. These aerials became another defin-
ing Dublin landmark, looking like a leafless forest as you entered
the city from the airport. The fringe reception wasn't all that hot;
one of our neighbours invited me in to see the World Cup final. I
think I saw Pele score for Brazil, but it was through what seemed
a snowstorm, so I can't be sure.

There I was, my exams all done at seventeen, and not a clue
where I was going from here. I didn't fancy three years of more
study at university for a degree, so, to avoid me getting under my
mother's feet, I went back to Belvedere and took a course in philosophy. I was young enough to still play schools rugby and feature
in the Gilbert and Sullivan, and it was a toff's life, lolling around
the classrooms without having to do homework or anything else
much. Too much of a good thing; I decided that my parents had
subsidised me long enough, and sat an exam for entry into the
Royal Bank of Ireland. Within a couple of months, I was behind a
desk in another classroom, learning how to count banknotes with
my left hand.

I spent four years as a bank clerk, four happy years, particularly when they transferred me to the Phibsborough or, as it was
known, Cattle Market branch. I could hop on a bus and get home

*The Capitol – just
one of the many cinemas
outside which I queued in
all weathers through the
fifties and sixties*

Two old ex-bankers, Leo Lacy and myself, reminisce about the good old days in the Royal Bank of Ireland

for lunch, and still be back in time, when the bank reopened for business at half-one. Ah, those were the days for clerking in the bank: open at ten o'clock in the morning, close at half-twelve, reopen at one-thirty and shut the doors again at three. Hardly consumer-friendly. You needed to be on your toes if you wanted to transact any business as a customer.

Throughout my briefly brilliant banking career, I never really regarded it as a proper job, when I thought of how hard my father worked, the hours he put in. We lesser lights of the Phibsborough branch, Royal Bank of Ireland, had usually wrapped up our minor tasks by a quarter past three, and were ready for the coffee shops and passing parade of Dublin's ultimate ambience of sophistication, Grafton Street. However, knowing that it would look bad if half the staff vacated the bank fifteen minutes after it had closed its doors, we contented ourselves with hard-fought games of shove ha'penny, until it was thought that we could decently take our leave, at a quarter to four.

Saturday was different. The bank kindly opened its doors to its customers from ten to half-twelve, a half-day. It was different for us, the supposed workers, as well: we could wear our rugby club tie, and a blazer. So, people could tell immediately if you were a Catholic or a Protestant, but only on the weekend. Given over to rugby, a few pints of Guinness in the clubhouse, off to some excuse for a restaurant to give the stout something to lie on (apart from a couple of expensive hotels, Dublin was a gastronomic sewer, then). And then, hit the tennis, or rugby, club hop. The girls had been there since eight, and in we'd walk, heavily redolent of stout and chips, and expect them to be pleased to dance with us. How did they put up with it? And then, we'd have the gall to be offended if the lassie we had chosen for our favours didn't select us for the 'ladies' choice'.

The most popular person at these 'hops' was the fellow with the car. I had a pal with such a vehicle, and it was a godsend: you didn't have to face a five-mile walk home, and you could offer a lift to the lucky lady of your choice. Unfortunately, it was never the back-seat romance you were hoping for; she always had a friend, plain, sulky and suspicious. No wonder sex was in its infancy in the Dublin of the fifties. Still, I didn't feel deprived – it was a grand life, on five quid a week, two pounds ten shillings of which I gave to my mother. The other two pounds ten shillings were given over to pleasure. Drink, dance, the pictures, and coffee in the Rainbow Café afterwards. Two and a half quid went a long way in those days.

Grafton Street, where the Ma and Da worked together, and fell in love. Dublin's smartest thoroughfare

You were all right as long as you got into the bank before half-nine. Otherwise, you'd be below a red line drawn in the attendance book, and subject to a reprimand from the manager, a man whose bark was worse than his bite and whose reputation as a disciplinarian was somewhat undermined by a suit made from hopsacking and the open sandals that he favoured. We'd hang around chewing the cud, until the manager shouted from his office, 'Is anybody going to open the bank today?', and up would spring the porter, a remarkable little man with a German name and a Scots accent. He opened and closed the place, first in, last out, fetching and carrying, relaying messages, and cooking the manager's lunch, a chop and vegetables. It was a task not in the porter's job description, but he told me that he took consolation in kicking the manager's chop around the floor before cooking it.

Wherever the porter was to be found in the bank, there could be heard the ringing sounds of trumpet, clarinet and trombone, French horn and flute. He had ambitions for the music hall, and a dream of a whole orchestra of musical impersonators, without an instrument between them. It never came to anything, not enough musical impersonators, I imagine, but it was a dull day indeed in the bank that the safe, or the kitchen upstairs, did not ring to some Dixieland favourite. A passer-by could be forgiven for thinking that Louis Armstrong was a customer...

The bank doors finally open, in they'd come: the man from the fish and chipper across the road, the pub owner from next door, the cattle-jobber, the farmer, and the pig-man. You could smell the pig-man long before he came through the door, and it must have surprised him that every time he came to make a lodgement, the place seemed deserted. For the clerks, the tellers and the cashier were all hiding below their desks, knowing full well the appalling state of the poor man's banknotes, and not wishing to smell like the wrath of God for the remainder of the day, not to mention the danger of foot and mouth disease. A deathly hush would descend, while the bemused pig-man looked around for some sign of other human life, broken only when the manager, disturbed by the unwonted silence, came out of his office, saw what was happening and shouted, 'Cash!'

It was an intimate place and we were all pals together, which

That's not me, or the manager, in front of the Royal Bank of Ireland, Phibsborough branch, Dublin. It's a kebab shop now…

Leo Lacy and me at the back of the bus, recalling how we carried thousands of pounds, unguarded, in broad daylight, back and forward to Head Office, for years without anyone even saying, 'Boo!'

sometimes led to a certain hooliganism: taking a lodgement from a pretty customer, you'd find yourself hit between the eyes with a wet sponge, flung by another teller. The only answer to this was to enter his cubicle while he was taking a lodgement and tear up his neatly arranged pile of new notes. And, speaking of notes, it was my task, twice a week, to carry a bag of five thousand pounds' worth of soiled banknotes to Head Office in Foster Place, College Green, Dublin, there to have them replaced by five thousand quid's worth of clean notes, which I carried back to Phibsborough in the same bag. My friend, Leo Lacy, who replaced me as general dogsbody when I left the bank, came over from England to join me on *Terry Wogan's Ireland*, so that the public would know that I wasn't making all this up, and he figured that, in today's

The bus route took me past the memorial to parliamentarian and nationalist, Charles Stewart Parnell, in O'Connell Street

money, we were carrying well in excess of fifty thousand pounds, both ways, twice a week, uninsured, unprotected, on a bus, which, naturally, we waited for in the ordinary way, at a bus stop. When I say 'unprotected', let's be fair: the bank porter was with me, carrying the bus fare.

Safely aboard, down Phibsborough Road, along Dorset Street, past North Great George's Street and Belvedere where I went to school, the Parnell Monument, the broad expanse of O'Connell Street and the historic post office, over the Liffey into D'Olier Street, past the Ballast Office clock that was an 'epiphany' to James Joyce, around Trinity College, which at the time you had to be a foreigner or an Irish Protestant to attend, unless you had a special dispensation from the all-powerful Archbishop of Dublin. I know, I know, but that's what we put up with then. On the right, the great pillared façade of the Bank of Ireland, the old Irish House of Parliament when Dublin was the second city of the British Empire, and then, the enclave of Foster Place. It wasn't a quiet journey – the porter took the opportunity to give me and the other bus passengers a selection of his musical impressions to while away the time. I thought it might be more suitable, given our task, if we kept a slightly lower profile, but he took the view that we'd be handing the money over to whoever asked, and running like hell anyway, so it didn't really matter.

Off the bus then, and through the dark doors of Head Office to the Note Department. The man in charge once showed me the gun he kept in his drawer, in case of trouble. It looked like something Wyatt Earp might have used at the O.K. Corral. We were out the door again in five minutes, with the new notes. In no hurry to get back to kicking the manager's chop about, or sorting florins from half-crowns, we would stroll, the porter and I, in a desultory manner, to Bewley's Oriental Café where the odours of freshly ground coffee beans would lure us in for a cup of Java and a bun. We would always place the money carefully under the table, and never once forgot it. It's extraordinary that nobody ever knocked us over; we never changed our routine or our route, walking about Dublin with all that money. It never occurred to me that, on a fiver a week, I might have done a runner myself, and even now, be writing this 'neath a palm tree on a tropical isle.

My social life was enhanced by a Morris Minor, my first car, generously donated by the Da, who got it from a friend of a friend, at the right price. There was no driving test in Ireland at the time, so, after a couple of lessons from a pal on the wide green expanse of Phoenix Park, I paid for a driving licence and I was on the road! No more traipsing the streets at all hours from hops and pubs, no more buses, goodbye bike. I could now range further afield, to far-flung ballrooms in Skerries or Bray, to barbecues on Killiney Beach, to house parties wherever they may be. It made little difference. The girls in the ballrooms still lugged their silent friends around for protection, the barbecues were all over bar a charred sausage and a lone guitarist by the time you got there, and I always ended up drinking in the kitchen at parties. The only really good party I ever went to was the one where I met Helen, but I don't want to get ahead of myself...

How I didn't turn into a bicycle, with all the cycling I did as a boy, I'll never know

My little Morris Minor had its flaws – a broken passenger seat (I've no idea), a dent on the front bumper matching the one on the boot, and a nearside indicator that had never worked, requiring elaborate circular arm motions through the driver's window that were supposed to indicate turning to the left. There was a perpetual slow puncture on the front nearside wheel, no surprise – it's a wonder they didn't all have a slow puncture, since all my tyres were 'remoulds'. No thinking motorist ever bought a new set of car tyres in Ireland. Nor did they ever buy a new car. Every other car in Ireland was a wreck. The Irish simply didn't care about their motor vehicles in the same way as the British. There was a theory that it was only the dirt that was holding most of the country's cars together.

The Irish farmer, in particular, made no distinction between his car and a pick-up truck. Exhausts were allowed to hang off, boots were only secured by knots of hairy twine. I've seen a calf in the back of a Ford Popular, a sheep in the front seat of a Fiat. Some years ago, the Irish police halted a car that was being driven even more erratically than normal. It was found to have kitchen chairs instead of front seats. Naturally their sliding back and forward on every hill and corner led to the eccentricity of the driving, but the driver was surprised to be dragged before the magistrates. He explained: 'Sure the car seats were so comfortable, we

Bewley's Oriental Café.
Ah, the smell of freshly
ground coffee

took 'em out and put them around the kitchen fire, and put the kitchen chairs in the front of the car.'

My great friend and mentor, the man who gave me my chance on radio, the late Denis Meehan, had not one, but two wrecks of cars parked in front of his house, just outside Dublin. Both had dead batteries, and required vigorous pushing by friends and family if you wanted to get anywhere. One evening, Denis was called out on an emergency by Radio Éireann, where he was Head of Presentation. No time for a friend's jump-leads charge-up, no time for a laborious push down the hill, so in desperation he ran into the road and waved down a passing car. He persuaded the lady driver to reverse back a couple of hundred yards and then drive into his old wreck to get it going down the hill and away. Then Denis got into his car, put her into first, and foot on the clutch, ready for the push. It was only when he looked in his rear-view mirror that he saw the other car racing towards his at about thirty miles per hour. He could only sit there, and brave himself. The damage was hardly noticeable on Denis's wreck, but the lady's car… She apologised profusely.

I get many letters every year from young people who want to

be radio and television presenters, and from the hundreds of degree courses in media studies that are conducted by Britain's universities it would appear that every second person who comes out of school with decent A levels wants to follow a career in the media and, for preference, in television and radio rather than print. You can't blame young people – the media seem more exciting than the professions, industry, science or the civil service. And you could get to become 'famous'! Fame's the spur that drives so many these days, whether it be on *The X Factor*, *Britain's Got Talent*, or writing to the likes of me to ask how they can get that big break. And how I wish I could tell them. For there's no ladder in my business, no clear career path, and no degree course in the media that's going to be much help. All I can offer by way of guidance is to try your luck with hospital or local radio, or work your way up in a small, independent television company, from tea-maker, to runner, to researcher, and then, who knows, you might get lucky.

For luck is the biggest single element in a career in radio or television. To get an opportunity, to have whatever it takes to take advantage of that opportunity, and to have somebody there who likes you, you need all that, and more luck. And anybody who succeeds in life, and in this bizarre business that I have found myself without much effort, and forgets what a vital part luck played in that success, is deluded, blinded by the false and fickle jade of 'fame'.

I'm always being asked how I got my lucky start. It was an advertisement in an Irish newspaper: Irish national radio, Radio Éireann, was seeking 'Announcer/Newsreaders'. Only those fluent in English and Gaelic need apply, and having a passing acquaintance with European languages. To this day, I don't know why I answered that advertisement. My Gaelic was no great shakes, my French and German schoolboy standard, my Italian and Spanish non-existent, apart from a certain capacity for mimicry. It was the job of a lifetime, and jobs in the Ireland of the sixties were thin on the ground. Half the briefless barristers, bored accountants and out-of-work graduates in the country would be applying. Why did I, a bank clerk with only an undistinguished leaving certificate and a half-finished course in philosophy, even bother? I had no chance.

Much later, dear Denis Meehan told me that there had been

Killiney Bay, looking across to Bray Head, ideal for beach barbecues. They say that the view vies with Sorrento

A boy broadcaster approaches the microphone...

ten thousand applicants for the job. How did I even get to be called for an audition? But there I was, sitting in a little room in the radio station in Dublin's post office, watching an audition script dance in front of my eyes. There were news items in English, passages in Gaelic, musical introductions in French, Italian and German. I didn't get out of breath, I wasn't nervous, I think that I even enjoyed it. I suppose I was delighted to have got that far and didn't expect to go any further.

I had made an excuse to the bank manager of having a dental appointment that morning, and after lunch there I was, back behind my desk, counting other people's money. All I had to do now was wait for the 'thanks-but-no-thanks' rejection slip, and a steady career in a permanent, pensionable position in the bank. A month or so later, I was back at Radio Éireann on an announcer/ newsreader training course, and unable to believe my luck. Every evening, for a month, I'd balance my books in the bank, play the statutory game of shove ha'penny and then down to the radio studios for three hours of training in the arcane arts of newsreading and announcing. There were six of us on the course, with not a law degree, accounting qualification nor a spoiled priesthood between us. I'm sure Denis Meehan, who was running the course, was trying to break the mould of Irish radio presentation, away from the sub-BBC Home Service stodge into which it had sunk.

I never confided in anybody about what I was doing of a weekday evening, again, I suppose, in case it all ended in disappointment, but the Ma and Da, as usual, were happy to let me go in whatever direction life was taking me. They must have been worried that I was putting my secure, permanent, pensionable position, my 'job for life', at risk, but they never let on.

At the end of the course, lightning struck again, and I was offered part-time work. So, once more, back to the bank, balance the books, shove the ha'penny, but this time sit in a darkened studio and wait for the green light to come on, then read the day's Cattle Market Report to an awaiting nation. How I got through the hoggets, the wethers and the fat-stock prices, I'll never know. I was fighting for breath from the first moment, the very ceiling seemed to be pressing down on me. The memory of that first five-minute broadcast is fresher in my mind than anything I've ever done on radio or television since.

Out of courtesy, and just in case things went pear-shaped in my new career as a boy broadcaster, I told my bank manager of my part-time job on the radio. He smiled indulgently – loads of people worked part-time at one thing or another at that time in Ireland, to keep body and soul together. I'm sure he put it down to a passing phase, a bit of youthful dilettantism; inconceivable that anybody with any sense would sacrifice security and respectability in the bank for the life of a roustabout and hobbledehoy. Then Radio Éireann offered me the job and I left, without a backward glance, deluded fool that I was, lured by the siren call of glamour, showbiz and fame.

I've told the story elsewhere of calling into a bank in Dublin about twenty-five years ago, when I had been lucky enough to enjoy success on British television and radio. I recognised the teller, as he cashed my cheque. He recognised me, too, but in that begrudging way that remains the least endearing quality of my people, he wasn't going to let on.

'There y'are,' he said. 'How's it goin'?'

'Oh, not bad,' I replied. 'How's yourself?'

'Pullin' the divil by the tail,' he answered. 'I should be full-time in the cash, next year. By the way, you joined the bank with Ray Murphy, didn't you?'

'Yes,' I said, 'nice fella. How's he doing?'

'Assistant manager in Schull, in Cork. You left at the wrong time...'

There's no pretending that leaving the secure portals of the Royal Bank was a reckless, buccaneering sortie into the great unknown on my part. Irish radio was a semi-state body – I might as well have joined the civil service. But the money! My first pay packet was £14 7s 2d a week, rising by annual increments of 12s 11d to £17 11s 8d at the top of the scale. I'd been earning £5 a week in the bank – it was a king's ransom, almost a bank manager's pay! As Muds, the Granny, would put it, I was 'on the pig's back'.

I don't remember my first morning as a radio announcer, but I doubt if they would have let me anywhere near the mircophone on my first day, to welcome the great Irish public, in Gaelic and English, to another day's transmissions from Radio Éireann. I found that broadcasting hours weren't all that different from banking. None of the twenty-four-hour service we get, like it or not, from television and radio these days. Irish radio opened at the respectable hour of seven-thirty, the streets of Dublin barely aired, closed at three o'clock in the afternoon, to give people time to catch their breath, reopened at five, with children's pro-grammes, and sent everyone to bed at eleven. The studios were entered through the side door of the post office, a lift took you to the third floor, you stepped out into RE's Reception. There, behind a desk, a comely receptionist, a couple of studio atten-dants in uniforms shiny with age, and in a chair in the corner, a member of the police Special Branch in plain clothes, awaiting his pension, carrying a revolver as old as himself and ready to use it in defence of any attempt by an illegal organisation to take over the radio station for their own nefarious purposes. He never had to draw his six-shooter; it was just for show. Even the biggest eejit in an illegal organisation would have known that, if he had managed to commandeer a studio, by the time he'd got just a couple of words of revolutionary protest out, they would have switched off the transmitter in the Dublin mountains.

I'll never forget the thrill of driving through Dublin's dark streets at seven in the morning (they're a lot less deserted these days), parking the old Morris Minor down the side street beside the pub; in the door, up in the lift, and down the narrow dark corridor that housed RE's studios and offices, and down the very end, the only lights those of the continuity suite, where I would search through the prayer book for a saint of the day, and, ready to take my chances in Gaelic with Saint Chrysostom, with a nod from the engineer, open the microphone and speak to the nation. They're listening to me! Little old me, the boy who didn't know what he wanted to do, the former bank clerk! The wonder, the thrill of it. I'd found something I could do, that I loved, that was going to be my life.

At the far end of the long corridor, beyond the bright lights and gaiety of the continuity suite, was a flight of stairs, and up there, in an attic of the post office, was the Radio Éireann newsroom, a veritable maelstrom of telex and typewriter, talk and cigarette smoke. I would perch prettily beside the senior sub-editor, who'd collate his newshounds' reports, and hand it over, or as much as was ready, to me, the gob on a stick, as all God-fearing news and sports journalists have referred to presenters since the beginning of time. Down the rickety stairs I'd go, and on the hour begin to read the news to the waiting Irish public.

Often, there would be only a couple of sentences to go before a great silence settled over the nation, when the door would swing open, and in would come Charlie, the sub-editor, with the rest of the news, or at least the next couple of pages to be going on with. It didn't suit Charlie, all that rushing up and down the stairs. He'd sit by me as I read, wheezing gently. You could say it was a good training ground for a novice newsreader, providing he didn't have a nervous breakdown. When people ask me where I found the nerve to present two hours of live radio every day on BBC Radio 2, I nod sagely and smile enigmatically. They should have been around Irish radio in the good old days.

You had to give them credit, whoever designed the rabbit

Jammet's Restaurant – a piece of Dublin that was forever Paris

warren that was Radio Éireann, husbanded the space, for there were studios upstairs as well, music studios. All very fine for fiddle, banjo, tin whistle, accordion and other portable instruments, but not so hot for double bass, harp or grand piano. Watching the elderly studio attendants trying to cart that stuff up those winding stairs brought into sharp relief what was meant by 'man's inhumanity to man'. I introduced many an Irish traditional music broadcast from those very studios. It was a multi-skilling task, not only requiring Gaelic from the announcer, but also that he sneak into the studio while the music was being played and slip a cushion under the fiddler's boot, with which he was hammering the floor.

If you turned right at Reception, there was another corridor, with more studios – the home of the Radio Éireann players. Acting's a tricky trade at best, and stability of tenure not its outstanding trait, certainly not in the Ireland of the fifties and sixties. There were the 'fit-up' tours, the Dublin Gate Theatre of Mac Liammóir and Edwards, the national theatre, the legendary Abbey, and a few little 'studio' theatres that only provided semi-pro work. Ireland has always been keen on theatre, but there simply wasn't enough regular work for her actors. The rep, therefore, had the pick of the crop, and a brilliant mixture it was: the best of the 'fit-up' tourers, former Restoration fops from the Gate, Dublin and Kerry accents mixing with the Gaelic from Galway. What a privilege to make the opening announcement, and then watch and listen to some of Ireland's greatest actors as they ran the gamut of Ibsen, Sheridan, O'Casey and Synge. Raffish characters, not above a swift pint across the road in the Tower Bar if they didn't feature until the second act.

The Tower Bar was directly across Henry Street from the entrance to RE, and was ever a pub more shrewdly placed. Some producers, script and feature writers must have done their best work for radio there, because few ever saw them leave it, even during what was known as 'The Holy Hour'. This blessed time was between two-thirty and three-thirty in the afternoon, when Ireland's pubs locked their doors in response to kindly legislation, designed to give the honest landlord and his staff a chance to clear the tables, tidy the floor, and maybe even have a quiet couple of moments of reflective peace, before the turmoil and the pint-pulling began afresh. So, the Tower Bar, in common with every other pub, shut its doors. With its clientele still inside. 'A drink while you're waiting, gentlemen?' was the civil inquiry.

The demon drink was certainly the curse of Irish radio – all that free time between news bulletins, and opening and closing announcements, between first and second acts, between rehearsal and performance. It was freely accepted that drink was taken before, during and after broadcasts. How often did I hear, 'Johnny, best announcer we've ever had, if it wasn't for the drink…'?

The Tower Bar was for drinking, as was Madigan's pub in Moore Street. At that time, mine host of the latter was Paddy Madigan, a fine rugby player, and a fellow Belvederian. Daily, he gave the lie to the idea that a middle-class, privately educated person could not give as good as he got from the terrible-tongued market-stall women who crowded his banquettes and downed his pints as quickly as he could pull them. When you wanted something to provide a little ballast, it was across O'Connell Street to Mooney's Bar and Lounge, there to dissect a scrawny chicken leg or an unsatisfactory, thinly sliced ham sandwich. To this day, my wife says that she's never seen anyone reduce a chicken leg to its bare essentials like me, but I had the training for it. Denis Meehan wasn't just a master teacher of the art of speaking on the wireless – his way with a chicken was of surgical brilliance. When all flesh was gone, he'd suck the bones.

Occasionally, when we were both on an evening duty, Denis and I would repair, in our ramshackle vehicles, to an out-of-town eatery, The Goat, for steak and chips. Truth be told, Dublin was a gastronomic wasteland in the fifties and sixties, good restaurants were rarer than hen's teeth, only to be found in the grander hotels. There was one marvellous old French restaurant, Jammet's, with waiters in black, with long white aprons, but it was well outside the price range of a boy broadcaster. Years on, when I was slightly more flush and wished to impress my beautiful new inamorata, Helen Joyce, international model, I broke into the piggy bank and took her to Jammet's.

It was exquisite, an unforgettable evening that we still remember, not least because it was enhanced by a chance encounter that we were thrilled to observe between the great Irish actor and famous Dublin boulevardier, Micheál Mac Liammóir, and an even greater star of the silver screen in the thirties, forties and fifties. Micheál, who you could always hear across a crowded room and, indeed, a busy street, shouted his delighted greeting, 'Don! Don Ameche!', and rushed to embrace his fellow thespian in the approved theatrical manner. Ameche looked a little foxed, I thought, probably never having met Mac Liammóir in his life, but responded like an old pro, with his trademark Hollywood smile. I'll tell you what, it made our evening – French cuisine, and dinner with the stars…

I'd always loved eating, even though Rose Wogan, the Ma, was never mistress of the skillet or pan, so I've no idea where I acquired my delight in what's known as 'fine dining', or, as *MasterChef* has it, 'a nice plate of food'. The usual choice for the

Temple Bar, Dublin – the focal point for stag weekends, the craic and the pint

starving radio announcer was a little place down a side street called the Trocadero, with a Greek owner but with mainly Italian culinary influences. I'll not forget an evening when Denis and I, having cogitated long and hard over the merits of cannelloni as against kebabs, then turned our critical eyes to the wine list. What to complement the food? A Merlot? A Shiraz? A hearty Chianti? The waiter had waited long enough. 'And what will it be for booze, gentlemen?' The Irish have never been cut out to be waiters, or, in those long-gone days, chefs. You could have potatoes chipped, mashed, boiled, in their jackets or roasted, but every other vegetable was reduced to liquid mush, and you were never offered fish. Under the rule of the Holy Catholic Church, we had no choice but to eat fish every Friday, and so, like anything that's compulsorily forced down your throat, nobody ever ate it any other day of the week.

Between one and three every weekday afternoon, Radio Éireann became a commercial broadcasting organisation, with a succession of fifteen-minute 'sponsored' programmes, consisting mainly of music and plugs for the product or company: Irish Fisheries, Jacob's biscuits, Donnelly's sausages, and a drama of everyday country folk, *The Kennedys of Castleross*, as successful at the time as *The Archers* on BBC Radio; so much so that I've completely forgotten the product it was supposed to be advertising. I'll never forget Donnelly's sausages, though. Not because of their quality – there were far superior sausages being made in Dublin by German émigrés, such as Hafner's and Youksetter. No, it was the commercial that made Donnelly's: 'So, the next time you visit your grocer, tell him only one sausage will do. To his other suggestions say, "No, sir!" It's Donnelly's sausage for you!' Nothing remarkable there, you cry, but it wasn't the song, it was the singer – Val Doonican. The next time I heard him on the radio was a

The Kennedys of Castleross. *A breeding ground for much of Ireland's acting talent, it was as popular in its time as that other tale of country folk,* **The Archers**

year or so later, with music and his relaxed charm on the BBC Light Programme, and then, all hell broke loose and, there he was, king of Saturday night on BBC Television.

The most popular radio programme of the day in Ireland was *Hospitals Requests*, and, glory be, it was part of the announcer's duties, strictly rotated. Some of the older members regarded it as a bit of a chore, sorting through thousands of cards and letters and building a two-hour music programme that went out live every Wednesday lunchtime. Then, as 'sponsored' programmes understood, lunchtime was the country's biggest listening time. Everybody in Ireland, from workers to schoolchildren, went home for lunch, and, of course, the lady of the house was already there. Nowadays, nobody's at home in Ireland for lunch.

For me, *Hospitals Requests* was the Holy Grail of broadcasting; an opportunity to stop enunciating, to talk to the listener like a human being, to risk making it up as I went along. I would have done it every week, given the chance. From the beginning, I realised that 'ad-libbing' of cards and letters was something I could do. An opinion not necessarily shared by everybody – a couple of years later, I came across a memo from a producer in Irish television: 'Don't let Terry Wogan ad-lib.'

The popularity of *Hospitals Requests* was based on the simple premise that it was the only programme on Irish radio where you could occasionally hear popular music. For the trouble with a 'request' programme is just that – the requests. I knew that if I left it to the great Irish listening public, I'd spend my time playing nothing but 'The Nun's Chorus', 'Blow the Wind Southerly', 'The Priest in His Boots' by the Tulla Céilí Band, and 'Bring Flowers of the Rarest' by Father Sydney MacEwan. Safe, Catholic and holy. Some years ago, my friend, Gay Byrne, invited me on his *Late Late Show* on Irish television, the world's longest-running chat show. Halfway through, he introduced a choir to sing the most-requested song on his radio show. It was 'Bring Flowers of the Rarest'... I knew then why I'd been right to leave when I did.

Whenever it was my turn on *Hospitals Requests*, I'd go through the cards until I came to one that didn't specify a choice of music, so I'd pick what I wanted. All my time was spent in the gramophone library, hour upon hour, when like any proper broadcaster I should have been talking rubbish in the snug of the Tower Bar. It was in flagrant contravention of everything the old programme stood for, but it began to garner at least one good opinion: 'A word of thanks to Terry Wogan. With his cheery, good-humoured banter, he has given this programme a new look. One listens to him as much as one does to the records.' An ex-patient.

Encouraged, I pressed on, with ever bolder, more modern music to delight the unwell and infirm. The Clancy Brothers and Tommy Makem had become popular, particularly in the States, with their brand of cheery, manly Irish balladeering, and I decided to include their latest record in the programme. A shame I didn't listen to it before I played it. For the second line of 'Isn't it Grand, Boys?' talks about being dead… Hardly the tone for the sick and their worried families. Another letter followed: 'What was the mentality of the friends of hospital patients when they requested such a song?' It wasn't helped by some of the other lines in the song, which refer to a coffin and the withered flowers upon it.

The Clancy Brothers and Tommy Makem. Their song, 'Isn't it Grand, Boys?', with its not-so-cheery lyrics, caused a bit of a stir when I played it on Hospitals Requests

Despite the eccentricity of mode of dress – he favoured a moth-eaten cardigan, through the holes of which he attached his braces to his trousers – his wrecked motors, and a habit of quoting freely from *At Swim-Two-Birds* by Myles na gCopaleen, Denis Meehan was an innovator. For thirty years or more, Radio Éireann had drifted along, a national radio station for Ireland, inspired by the mother of all broadcasters, the BBC, and its Home Service. Its programmes were well-meaning, diverse in music and drama, but overloaded with the Irish language which most people didn't know much, and couldn't care less about. And talk. Tedious, endless talk. Denis was determined to bring RE, or at least his little bit of it, Presentation, into the middle of the twentieth century. So he added Andy O'Mahony, Gay Byrne, me, and at least three other young part-timers to his roster, which included half a dozen thirty- or forty-year-olds. It's a tribute to that Irish willingness to avoid confrontation and get on with each other, at least when face to face (when the back is turned, it's not necessarily the same), that young and old rubbed along together, with nary a cross word.

Naturally, young blood brought with it high spirits, and a fine disregard for the air of solemnity that pervaded RE at that time. I have been foully slandered by my fellow young announcer/

newsreaders as the instigator, nay ringleader, of such inappropriate diversion. I have no recollection of setting fire to a fellow announcer's script, from the bottom up, as he set the scene for *Die Fledermaus*. Nor, indeed, the pouring of a carafe of water slowly over someone's head, as they read the one o'clock news. And, if it comes to that, it wasn't me who sought to unbutton a lady announcer's blouse, as she was giving her all to the Cattle Market Report.

My friend, and fellow boy broadcaster of the sixties, Brendan Balfe, claims that one afternoon, fed up with having to close down the radio station at three o'clock when we could be reflecting the Swinging Sixties with some music, on the foolish notion that it might be better to keep our audience listening, I said, 'We're closing down now until our children's programmes at five o'clock. If, however, you'd like to keep listening, the BBC Light Programme is broadcasting some popular music, which you might enjoy. But be sure to join us again at five.' I deny it, categorically.

Although I can't deny another Balfe story about me, which he recounts in his excellent autobiography, *Radio Man*. It was a couple of years on, I had become a familiar face on the now Irish television service, RTE, and had just met Helen. In the usual attempt to impress, I had taken her to the Shelbourne Hotel's swanky Horseshoe Bar, soigné haunt of Dublin's smart set. We hardly noticed two ladies of the night, negotiating with a couple of visiting gentlemen. Negotiations came to naught, unfortunately, and the two ladies huffily made their way to the door. Not before they spotted me. 'Ah! Looka! There's Terry Wogan!' exclaimed the first. 'Thinks he's effin' gorgeous,' replied the second. Helen and I received the full attention of the Horseshoe Bar, while the dry martinis melted in our hands.

By then, I should have become inured to the Irish public's habit of expressing their opinions of the great and good in public, and loudly: 'That's Terry Wogan!' 'Oh yeah. Very fat, isn't he?' Or another young lion of Irish television at the time, Mike Murphy, sipping a reflective Guinness in his local when a passing Jackeen spots him: 'Mike Murphy! I think you're effin' awful!' Before Mike can riposte, the man leaves through the swing doors. Only to burst through them again: 'And the wife thinks you're effin' awful, as well. And she knows eff-all!' Hard to finish a pint with any dignity in those circumstances.

It's not just eejits like myself, mere hobbledehoys who happen to have caught the public's attention, that the Irish feel free to use as Aunt Sallys. Everybody comes in for their share of jeering and abuse: the recently departed Taoiseach, Brian Cowen, was known to all and sundry as 'Biffo' (Big Ignorant F–r from Offaly); the legendary Eamonn de Valera was 'The Long Fella'; but it was the Irish public's cavalier treatment of another president, Sean T. O'Kelly, that seemed the cruellest. As is the tradition to this day, the President is presented to both teams before an international rugby match. Sean T. was a dapper man, in homburg hat and Crombie coat, but not the tallest. As he was led out on to the field by two large aides-de-camp to meet thirty enormous rugby players, the crowd would shout, as one voice: 'Cut the grass! Cut the grass!' I hardly need to explain the implication, but it demonstrates the Irish public's singular lack of respect for anybody who thinks that they're better than them, or authority generally.

The praising with faint damns is another characteristic common to the Irish, identified by the great broadcaster, Alistair Cooke. He remarked that the best conversations anywhere were to be heard in Dublin pubs – Davy Byrne's, McDaids, Neary's. Alistair claimed that he could hear them still, although back in Manhattan. The conversation would be as follows:

'Did you meet that Alistair Cooke the other week?'

'Ooh, don't be talking to me,' would come the reply. 'What a man! What a talker! And the turn of phrase!'

Another voice: 'You wouldn't hear the like of it anywhere.'

'And a fine-lookin' man – such knowledge of the arts and literature!'

'A great man altogether!'

And then, recounted Cooke, there'd be a pause, while the men supped their stout. Then, a voice: 'Do you mind the way he picked his nose?'

I was part of the commentary team for the funeral of Sean T. O'Kelly, perched in the third-storey window of a flat in Dorset

The General Post Office, historic site of the 1916 Easter Rising, where, as W.B. Yeats said, 'a terrible beauty was born'

Street, the better to describe the cortège as it made its slow, sad way to what they used to call 'The Dead Centre of Ireland', Glasnevin Cemetery in north Dublin, where a tall, round tower marks the grave of 'The Liberator', Daniel O'Connell. Sean T., for all the jeering at his small stature, was much loved as 'a decent little man', and the Irish love a funeral. It's one of the attributes of my people that they attach as much importance to a final farewell to a friend or relative, as they do to a christening, or a wedding.

John F. Kennedy brings his magnetism to Dublin and, like every American President since, discovered his Irish roots

I was privileged to play a role, too, in the biggest ever outside broadcast staged by Radio Telefís Éireann – the visit to Ireland by President John F. Kennedy in June 1963. The President of the USA was touring Europe and, in the interest of many millions of Irish votes in the States, was paying homage to his Irish roots, by visiting the land of his forefathers, and particularly the little cottage in Wexford from where the Kennedys began their long journey from starvation to the Land of the Free. This time, my commentary position was at the bottom of Dame Street, to catch and colour the moment as the President's motorcade passed by on its journey from Dublin airport, through the centre of the city, before crossing the Liffey, and then on to Áras an Uachtaráin, the Irish president's residence, in Phoenix Park. I could see the motorcade, John F. Kennedy standing up in his open car to acknowledge the cheers of the enthusiastic crowd, as it swung into College Green, past the historic façades of the Bank of Ireland and Trinity College, founded by Queen Elizabeth I.

This was a big moment for a boy broadcaster; the commentator who had been covering the procession from O'Connell Bridge to College Green handed over to me. 'Thank you, Padraig. Yes, the motorbike outriders swing into this historic part of Dublin, and there, the young president, smiling as he waves to the cheering thousands! And there he goes, and I hand you over to Seán

Murphy.' For, as the mighty motorcade swept into College Green, through my binoculars I saw John F. tap his driver on the shoulder. They shot down the street, and past me, in about twenty seconds. My greatest broadcasting moment to date, passing by as the idle wind…

The General Post Office, in which was housed the rabbit warren that was Radio Éireann, is the most important building in Irish history. It was here, in 1916, that a small band of brave men declared an Irish Republic, flinging their stand for independence in the face of the greatest empire in the world. The proud declaration of that Republic can be seen on a plaque within the main hall, by the bronze statue of the great mythological hero, Cúchulainn. In this place, Patrick Pearse and his Volunteers, joined by James Connolly and his Citizen Army, fought their hopeless battle, before being overwhelmed by 'Britannia's sons,

Dublin Castle. From here, the British ruled Dublin, and Ireland

with their long-range guns'. The GPO, and much of O'Connell Street, was reduced to rubble, and the leaders of the rebellion, known forever afterwards as 'The Easter Rising', were taken out and shot. It was those executions of brave men, who knew that their uprising would lead inevitably to their death, that gave birth to what the poet W.B. Yeats called 'a terrible beauty' that struck at the minds and hearts of every Irishman, and led inexorably to Ireland's real independence in 1921.

On the fiftieth anniversary of that Easter Rising, RE marked the occasion with another mammoth outside broadcast, particularly plucky for a television service that had barely got off the ground. Once again, despite not having much to say for myself on President Kennedy, I was selected to commentate on the celebrations to commemorate the great sacrifices made at the GPO. This time, my vantage point was position 'A', directly opposite the pillars of the post office, on the other side of O'Connell Street. My task was to describe the march-past of Ireland's finest: army and navy, as the air force swept above, proudly marching past the very spot where 'terrible beauty' and the country's ultimate independence were born.

The parade started at the former seat of British power, Dublin Castle. I could hear my fellow commentators describing the majesty of the parade, although it must be said here that the Irish Republic has never been big on military might, with a small professional army and a navy that at the time boasted two old World War Two corvettes, for protection of the coastal waters. Nonetheless, it was a proud and colourful show, with the Number One Army Band playing mightily. My job was to describe the parade as it marched past the focal point, the General Post Office, and I'd fully briefed myself on the dignitaries who would be taking the salute. The President was there, and the Prime Minister, a couple of prominent politicians and, of course, the Archbishop of Dublin, but of the rest of the country's great and good, whose proud names and honours I had fully documented, in front of me there was no sign.

Later, it transpired that their invitations had not been received, or, possibly, even despatched. So they filled up the empty places on the reviewing stand with passers-by, who were, I'm sure, grateful

The Easter Rising. 'Britannia's sons, with their long-range guns, sailed in through the foggy dew' – and quelled the rebellion that became the catalyst of Irish independence

for the opportunity to sit down and applaud the parade from the best seat in the house. It wasn't easy, but I chuntered on until the parade passed by, freely identifying the dignitaries who weren't there.

There I was, having the time of my life, my feet barely under the radio announcer's table, but 'the times they were a-changin''. The biggest upheaval in Irish life since the Declaration of Independence, the new Irish television service! Of course, everybody in the country had known that it was coming – Eamonn Andrews, Ireland's most famous broadcaster, a huge star on BBC TV and Radio, had been appointed Chairman of the new Radio Telefís Éireann Authority, studios were being built in Montrose, on Dublin's more respectable south side, staff were being recruited. Anybody with any television experience was in, and so they came, on every mail boat, from Britain, Canada, the States, as far afield as Australia. People who had been studio attendants, scene shifters, cleaners at the BBC, ITV, NBC, CBS, or local television Alice Springs, overnight became floor managers, senior cameramen, directors and producers. Meanwhile, I failed the audition to become a television newsreader. So did Andy O'Mahony. Never mind; such was the confusion that reigned, Andy and I were

Patrick O'Hagan and the Number One Army Band braving the snowballs being hurled at them on RTE's opening night

reading the news on RTE six months later. An American came out of nowhere, this time not to be an ordinary producer/director, but Director General.

RTE was ready and raring to go, and it did, on New Year's Eve 1962, from the ballroom of the Gresham Hotel, one of Ireland's finest, on Dublin's grandest thoroughfare, O'Connell Street. Only Irish flair and bravado, the 'let's give it a lash!' mentality, could have thought for a minute that an untried, untested television service, operated by untried, untested personnel, could possibly launch itself with a major outside broadcast. If just one little plug had come out of one little socket... But as the snow came down, the lights went up and all was glitter and glamour, as Eamonn Andrews declared Ireland's new television service open for the country's approval and delight. I wasn't asked; I was reading the news that night on the radio.

Eamonn Andrews. Ireland's own – the most popular broadcaster of his day in Britain, and first Chairman of RTE

The RTE Concert Orchestra played some fine Irish airs for the distinguished and select invitees, and two of the country's finest tenors, Brendan O'Dowda and Patrick O'Hagan, sang Irish ballads. Brendan was the luckier – he was inside, out of the weather, hands in pockets as usual, singing a selection of Percy French crowd-pleasers. O'Hagan was on the stand outside, accompanied by the Number One Army Band, with 'Danny Boy' and 'They're Cutting the Corn Around Creeslough Today'. Patrick was wrapped against the driving snow, with what looked like an army greatcoat over his dinner jacket. Even as he tried to sing, the Dublin public, with that splendid disregard for personality or occasion that I have already referred to, threw snowballs. They came from all directions, striking bassoons and trumpets, flutes and drums, even the conductor, who luckily had his back to the assault. O'Hagan was not so lucky, suffering some direct hits that effectively stopped 'Danny Boy' in his tracks, hardly making it to 'the pipes, the pipes are calling'. The conductor visibly staggered under a volley of snow on the back of his neck, and somebody took the decision that they might be better off in the safety and warmth of the Gresham ballroom. Mild panic ensued, but the bold Eamonn ad-libbed, while the orchestra were dragged back from the bar, Brendan was persuaded to give another few bars of a song, and the opening night of Irish television carried on...

The radio news, so happy in its little eyrie in the roof of the GPO, was moved to join the television newsroom at the almost-finished, shiny new studios in Montrose. The lads seemed happy enough with the open plan, but for the poor announcer/newsreaders, it was a two-way street. Radio programmes still came from the dusty corridors of the third floor of the post office – radio being now the poor relation, a start had yet to be made on its studios. When they were eventually built, they were in the basement. Why poor, sad radio presenters are expected to give their all while facing a brick wall is something I will never understand, having suffered such privation for years, not only on Irish radio but at the BBC too.

Anyway, the announcer's lot on what was now RTE was not a happy one, presenting programmes and working in the continuity suite at the old stand in Henry Street, but having to traipse across town to Montrose to read the news. Taxing on my little Morris Minor, with its remoulded tyres and dodgy exhaust, but not without its excitement of being part of a bustling, new, television newsroom. The radio news was now read from a little studio just off the newsroom. Once again, security, and the fear of the IRA charging up the stairs out of nowhere and commandeering the microphone, meant precautions had to be taken. The newsreader was required to lock himself, and his bulletin, in the little studio, with no regard for his claustrophobia, and wait for the red light (all the way from the GPO).

Meanwhile, outside sat an old IRA man, now a member of the Special Branch of the Garda Síochána, with a large Smith & Wesson revolver prominently displayed about his belt buckle. 'Bat' was my favourite, nearing retirement, a man who had fought on the Republican side during the Civil War of the twenties, provoked by the signing of the 'Partition' Treaty, against the Free State government. The government side won, but its great hero, Michael Collins, was killed in an ambush, and Eamonn de Valera, who led the Republican side, eventually became Taoiseach, and then President. Bat had no great love for his former leader, 'that long drink of water up in the Park', but in fairness, the Irish have always preferred their heroes to be at a distance, or dead.

De Valera, 'Dev', kept Ireland out of World War Two, leading

Kinsale

Kinsale is a lovely place, more like a Cornish harbour town than an Irish one, and in my early days in Irish television I took great delight in sampling the local seafood, and trying to catch some of it, specifically, shark. Now, to catch your shark is not just a matter of hurling a line with a hook into the sea and hoping to come up with a great white. The sharks around Kinsale are 'basking' sharks, and no fools. They must be lured, by a disgusting mixture of entrails, called locally 'rubby dubby'. And if the rocking motion of the boat didn't cause you to throw up, the appalling smell of the rubby dubby certainly would make even the sturdiest stomach rumble. I caught a shark, but it was never recorded for the documentary I was making, not to mind posterity, as the cameraman was rendered sick as a dog in the well of the boat. I suppose it's enough to know that I did it, but it would be nice if I could find anybody who'll believe me.

The last time I was in Kinsale, it was just as lovely and still a place for oysters, prawns and, I suppose, the occasional shark. These days, I settle for a mackerel. Cork, of course, is not short of scenic beauty; the west of the county has become a haven for English, German and Dutch people who come as tourists and

The waters off Kinsale, scene of my great shark triumph – sadly unrecorded for posterity

The delightful harbour of Kinsale, fishing port, tourist town and gastronomic temple

remain, to enjoy the easier pace of life and the gentle coastline, kissed by the Gulf Stream. You'll find palm trees and tropical plants growing in Bantry and Glengariff, the beneficiaries of a warm current flowing all the way from the Caribbean which also bestows on Ireland its temperate, mild climate. And is the reason, as I've said before, why nobody comes to Ireland for the sunshine.

to its isolation for years afterwards, not helped by its leader's propensity towards insularity. Dev was a believer in Sinn Féin, meaning 'Ourselves Alone', and his philosophy was expressed in what he called his 'dream for Ireland' – a rural community of devout Catholics, each with their own whitewashed, thatched cottage and vegetable garden, the kettle on the hob over a turf fire to warm the old folk, while manly young men and modest women found their pleasure dancing at the crossroads... If ever there was a recipe for economic suicide. A direct result of this myopia was a devout people without work, and emigration continued until the nineties, when the roar of the Celtic Tiger was heard throughout the land.

Back in the little news studio, locked in, our hero begins to read the one o'clock news, a half an hour long, the major bulletin of the day for the Irish, most of whom, as we've already established, are at home for lunch. Five minutes in, and it's going as well as can be expected, when the first drops of my life's blood begin to fall and obliterate the page in front of me. The drops fall more freely; wipe, speak, wipe, kill microphone for a second, big wipe – the news must go on, even if I bleed to death! Turn off the mike again, stick corner of handkerchief up nose to staunch flow, mike on, read on! Hold hanky with left hand, turn over page with right. I'm on my own, bleeding to death, behind a locked door, with no hope of help, least of all from a man with a gun, on the other side of the door, who has no idea of the tragedy being enacted in the little studio, and is half-asleep anyway.

News over, I stagger, blood-boltered, from the studio. Of sympathy, from the boys on the news desk, there is none, merely the laughter of hooligans, with comments such as: 'We thought you were a bit nosy for the last twenty minutes...' People sometimes ask how I coped with the strain and stress of two hours of live, unrehearsed broadcasting every morning for years on BBC Radio 2. I merely nod, sagely. It was nothing, compared to nearly bleeding to death, live on the air.

So, there I was, a formerly faceless wonder of the radio, all over Ireland like a cheap suit. Letters began to creep into the newspapers: 'The Man I Would Most Like To Be With On A Desert Island: Terry Wogan, Telefís Éireann newscaster, the most

Hosting the popular quiz show, Jackpot – *'Spin the wheel, Suzanne!'*

attractive man I know, with his gorgeous smile…' A newspaper critic, obviously not the full shilling, described me as 'a debonair, competent TV newsman on top of his job'. I was twenty-four and, in Ireland at least, famous. Fame, as the television series told us, costs. Particularly if you were playing rugby on a Saturday afternoon. I was quickly singled out as a suitable subject for gouging, kicking and mauling, not, I think, because the louts were critical of my television performance, but rather to have the satisfaction of being able to say: 'Do you see that eejit reading the news? I gave him that black eye.' Then I tore a ligament, played again too soon, wrecked a cartilage – 'It fell out in bits in my hand,' said the kindly surgeon – and my rugby-playing days were over.

So were my palmy days as a lounge lizard! Very shortly I found it difficult to go for a sociable pint in one of the newly fashionable 'lounges' where Dublin's young adults congregated to eye each other up. It is not the Irish way to ignore those who have been foolish enough to put their heads above the parapet, so I found myself accosted, either by those who wished to indulge in a bout of fisticuffs to see who was the better man, or by the sycophants, whose two-faced fawning was even harder to take.

As they say, 'God never closes one door but he shuts another', and my television star was in the ascendant. I did a documentary on Kinsale, near Cork, a former fishing village, which had become the centre of the country's gastronomy. A historic place, too, because it was here, in 1601, that the two rebellious Ulster earls, O'Neill and O'Donnell, hoped to drive a stake through the heart of English power in Ireland, with the help of an expeditionary force from Spain, Philip, the Spanish king, being just as keen to give Elizabeth I one in the eye. It ended, as all these futile expeditions, including the Armada, did, with a crushing victory for the English, as a force led by General Mountjoy destroyed the army of O'Neill and O'Donnell, before they could even link up with the Spaniards. The Spanish force was allowed to sail back where they came from, and the two Ulster chieftains left Ireland, never to return. It became known in Irish history as the 'Flight of the Earls'; some say that the defeat marked the beginning of the end for 'Gaelic' Ireland. It probably was the catalyst for the English plantation of the country's most rebellious province, Ulster, Northern Ireland, with English Protestant and Scottish Presbyterian settlers, the consequences of which were suffered for over four hundred years.

The colourful, inviting streets of Kinsale – a fisherman's, and gastronome's, paradise

One of the more popular shows on the new Irish television service was a quiz, *Jackpot*. It was presented by Gay Byrne, the only presenter on RTE who actually knew what he was doing, having enjoyed success in Manchester with Granada Television. His workload in Britain became too much, so they gave the gig to Mr 'Debonair'. Unlike Gay, I hadn't a clue what I was doing, and it being the early days of RTE, neither did anyone else. My first live (everything was live – recording tape cost money) show didn't exactly set the heather blazing. An Irish newspaper TV critic was unusually kind: 'Terry Wogan's debut in *Jackpot* nearly ended in a debacle after the time-up signal failed to ring a bell for him… There was something extraordinarily insensitive in the way he was left to appear in vision as suffering from a first-night blackout.'

Despite the near-disaster, the show continued its run, and its success, regularly topping the ratings. It continued to have its mini-crises: if a contestant answered the general knowledge question correctly, they could 'Delete or Dip' – that is, wipe out the other competitor's point, or dip into the little box in front of them for a prize. The lady gets the question right – 'Delete or Dip, Nora?' 'I'll dip,' says she. 'Open the box!' I cry. 'There's nothin' in here,' says she. 'There must be!' says I. 'No,' says she, 'nothin'.'

It grew quiet; after a minute that seemed more like a lifetime, the production secretary came clattering down the ladder from the control room with the prizes she had forgotten to put in the boxes. And people ask me if I ever get nervous coping with the unexpected on *Children In Need*. I suppose my experiences on live television in Ireland armoured me for my career in Britain, but there's nothing like doing it live. You never have to look at it, it has to be done in the allotted time, and there's no use talking about it when it's over, it's on its way to the wide blue yonder; you might as well go home and have your dinner.

Then came the 'vertical plan', the brainchild of a new Controller of Programmes, a Swedish-American, Gunnar Rugheimer. The vertical plan had two important factors going for it: 1) nobody knew what was meant by it; and 2) it made everything else seem horizontal. These things are important, in television. The idea was to give every evening (RTE didn't start transmitting until five in the afternoon) a character, and a host of its own. And I was to be Mr Friday Night. Every Friday, the unfortunate Irish viewer would have me on their screen, describing the delights of the evening that lay ahead. If there was a live entertainment to present, I was your man. And in between programmes, I was to present brief magazine items: comedy, music, an interview. I think they paid me about thirty-five quid for the night.

Since meticulous preparation was never my forte, nor, indeed, that of the new television service, these 'magazine' items tended to come in on a wing and a prayer, and only the talents of such as Eamonn Morrissey and Frank Kelly kept alive the comedy cameos. The musical interludes were more predictable. Except for one Friday at about seven, when I introduced a lovely young singer-guitarist, perched fetchingly on a stool. Even as I spoke her name, I heard a crash, and out of the corner of my eye, there she was on the studio floor, guitar, stool and all. Naturally the camera stayed on me. The floor manager gave me two fingers, not by way of a critique but to tell me that I had two minutes to fill while they rebuilt the stool, the guitar and the girl.

You haven't experienced the feeling of the great void that opens up in a television presenter's brain when asked to speak for two minutes without a thought in his head. No autocue, of course:

RTE wasn't made of money. The guitar was banjaxed, they never got the unfortunate girl back on her stool, and don't ask me what I spoke about for the best part of five minutes, but it took me years to get over it, and learn again how to relax in front of a television camera.

The Irish broadcasting I left behind in late 1969 was still bedevilled by the big 'C's: Conservatism and Catholicism. Everything had to be scripted, edited and rehearsed, with little room for spontaneity and freedom of expression. Controversy and confrontation were non-existent, presenters and interviewers stuck to the straight and narrow, played the party game. The greatest change in Ireland over the past twenty years that I've observed has been in radio and television. Radio, in particular, has become radicalised; the 'phone-in' is king of the airwaves, and no opinion is too outrageous. British radio comes nowhere close to the forth-right views on everything from sex to religion expressed every day on Irish broadcasting. Local radio plays its part too, and I'm sure that it's not true that the most popular programme on those smaller stations is the six o'clock reading of the death notices... I think it marvellous that staid old Radio Éireann has become the great forum of Irish public opinion, and helped free the country from the small-minded parochialism, the prejudice that held it back for so long.

One of the people who can take the credit for breaking the mould is my friend Gay Byrne. For more than thirty-seven years he hosted *The Late Late Show*, and it could be said that the pro-gramme has been the biggest catalyst for change in modern Ireland. When Gay started to introduce mildly controversial sub-jects, in the seventies, all hell broke loose. People walked out of the studio, because the possibility of divorce being legalised in Ireland was discussed. Views on homosexuality and contracep-tion provoked outrage and apoplexy. Such reactions carried on well into the eighties, according to Gay, and indeed I'd say there's still a strong undercurrent of conservative, Catholic opinion that would rather the world, and particularly Ireland, stay in its little isolated backwater forever.

By the time Gay Byrne had finished with the *Late Late* it was featuring lesbian nuns, women's rights, abortion and AIDS specials. It helped drag Irish people, some of them still kicking and screaming, into the twenty-first century.

Somewhere out there, in the great blue yonder, the shade of dear, departed Denis Meehan must be smiling. He knew that change had to come, not only to Irish broadcasting, but to the country itself.

Even in the best of all possible worlds, change is not always for the best. As another Irishman, Oscar Wilde, put it, 'Be careful what you wish for'...

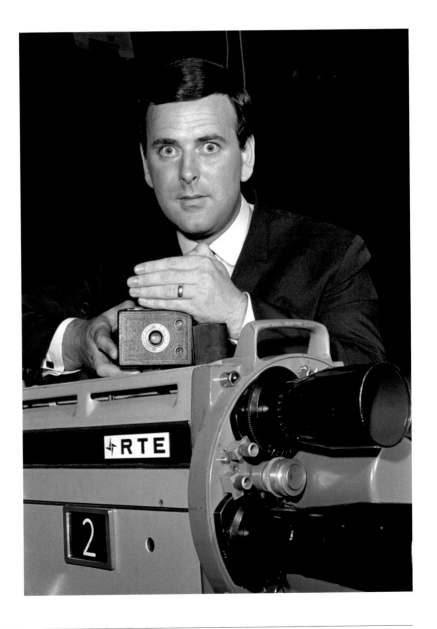

Comments are superfluous...

"A potent symbol of reconciliation – 'Hands Across the Divide' welcomes you to Derry/Londonderry"

...So I'll finish

So, while Northern Ireland seems to breathe more easily, as decades of violence come to what everybody in these islands hopes will be a final, peaceful end, the Republic finds itself on an economic roller-coaster ride. Although a country that survived eight hundred years of oppression, colonisation, discrimination, starvation and emigration should be able to handle most things fate can throw at it, the worldwide banking collapse has dealt my country a grievous blow.

The Ireland I left in the sixties was a country just beginning to get to its feet; the previous neutral, isolationist policy, Sinn Féin – 'Ourselves Alone' – leaving it largely reliant on agriculture and the small farmer, with unemployment, hardly any industry and the historical curse of emigration. Things didn't go much better for

Lunchtime in The Kitchen Bar, a Belfast institution. The Irish fondness for the pint is as famous as the Irish pub has become in cities all over the world

the next twenty years, unfortunately. Indeed, by 1988, the country was in dire economic straits, with the IMF – International Monetary Fund – breathing heavily down its neck.

However, and let's not forget how quickly economic fortunes may change, within a scant five years, a combination of the force of the European Community and shrewd tax incentives attracted huge inward investment (with only one per cent of Europe's population, Ireland was receiving ten per cent of all its international investment). Per capita of population, Ireland was suddenly Europe's most successful country – the Celtic Tiger. First came the information technology companies and then, as they found things even cheaper in India and the Far East, came Ireland's real boom: building and property. Housing prices sky-rocketed, everyone wanted a piece of the action, as the banks threw money around like sailors on shore leave. Irish investors borrowed and bought property from London to Courchevel, from the Mediterranean to the Black Sea.

The Irish had never had it so good, it was never going to end. Then the whole façade collapsed like a house of cards, all of it built on the fantasy of borrowed money. Three years on, Ireland's economic gloom seems worse than ever, recession turning inexorably into depression.

But these people, this island, have a history that puts the present sad situation into proportion. There's an Irish saying (isn't

ABOVE AND ABOVE LEFT: *There may be turbulent times ahead but the Irish spirit shines through, in music, song, dance, the craic – the simple joy in life and the living of it*

there always?), 'We saw the two days', meaning we had it good, and now things are not so hot. As I hope I've shown, there's still laughter here, and music, a joy in life and the living of it.

How can you even imagine that Ireland and the Irish will not rise again?

INDEX

Author's acknowledgements

Thanks to RDF (now Zodiak) Television, who got it off the ground;
Teresa Watkins, Martyn Ingram, the BBC's Maxine Watson.
To: Francine Lawrence, Lorraine Jerram, Luigi Bonomi.
To: Christopher Bruce, Oona O Beirn, Rob Goldie, the TV production team.
And, of course, to Helen and my family, without whom…

Picture credits

With thanks to Sir Terry Wogan for all the photographs he has kindly
supplied from his personal collection, and cameraman Rob Goldie for all
the digital images from the series *Terry Wogan's Ireland*.

We would also like to thank the following: **AIB Group** 182 top; **Alamy**
/Design Pics Inc 13, 18, 50–51, /Kevin Galvin 212, /Jack Macguire 120–121,
/Peter McCabe 23, /Mary Evans Picture Library 147 right, /Barry Mason
183, /George Munday 95, /Stephen Power 63, /Robert Harding Picture
Library 2; Corbis /Atlantide Phototravel 68–69, 70–71, /Bettmann 198,
/Chris Hill Photographic 146, /Richard Cummins 46 bottom, 176–177, 220,
/EPA/STR 131, /Eye Ubiquitous/Hugh Rooney 10–11, /Tim Graham 54,
/Hulton-Deutsch Collection 176, /The Irish Image Collection/Design Pics
73, 77, /Loop Images/Ros Drinkwater 219, /Douglas Pearson 112–113,
/Radius Images/Siephoto 208–209: **Courtesy Fáilte Ireland** 27, 34–35, 122–
123, 169, 175 left, 208, 220–221; **Getty Images** /Express Newspapers 138,
/Harrison 206, /Hulton Archive 44, 204, /Keystone 202, /F J Mortimer 147
left, /Time & Life Pictures/Hans Wild 192; **Ilex – Urban Regeneration
Company** 132; **Irish Jesuit Archives** 93; **www.jameshoranshootspeople.
com** 118–119; **The Kennelly Archive** 82–83, 85; **Lebrecht Music & Arts**
/Graham Salter 24 top; **Mary Evans Picture Library** 20–21; **Courtesy of
The National Library of Ireland** 39, 46 top; © **2011 – Northern Ireland
Tourist Board** 125, 142–143, 152–153, 155, 158–159, /Brian Morrison 8–9,
74–75, 134–135, 137, 145, 150–151; **Photolibrary.com** /Britain on View/
Tony Pleavin 140–141 top, /Richard Cummins 96, 180–181, /Eye Ubiquitous
65, /Hoffmann Photography 60–61, /Imagebroker.net 43, 110–111, /The
Irish Image Collection 15, 17, 30–31, 33, 40–41, 48–49, 53, 57, 76, 89, 100–
101, 109, 115, 160–161, 163, 173, 185, 187, 200–201, /John Warburton-Lee
Photography/Paul Harris 216–217, /Loop Images 103, 128, /David Lyons 68,
78–79, /Radius Images 66–67, /SGM 4, /Tetra Images 170–171, /Tips Images
203, /The Travel Library/Frank Fell 175 right; **Tourism Ireland** /Jonathan
Hession 81, /Chris Hill 99, 164, /Holger Leue 195; © **RTÉ Stills Library**
98, 178, 184, 188, 196, 205, 211, 215; **Rex Features** /Mike Webster 133.